Italian Aces
of World War 1

SERIES EDITOR: TONY HOLMES

OSPREY AIRCRAFT OF THE ACES • 89

Italian Aces of World War 1

Paolo Varriale

OSPREY
PUBLISHING

Front cover
Ranking Italian ace Maggiore Francesco Baracca of *91ª Squadriglia* obtained his 34th, and final, victory on 15 June 1918 whilst at the controls of SPAD VII S2445 during the fierce aerial dogfights on the first day of the last Austro-Hungarian offensive against Italian forces defending the River Piave. At 1300 hrs, Baracca had shot down a Hansa-Brandenburg Br C I two-seater of *Fliegerkompagnie* (*Flik*) 32/D near Saletto for his 33rd success. Flying with his veteran wingman Sergente Gaetano Aliperta, Baracca subsequently wrote in his combat report;

'We spotted a great patrol of 25 fighters flying at a height of about 1200 m. They chased our aeroplanes for a short while, then headed back toward their lines. One of them had drifted away from the patrol, and we quickly surrounded it. I repeatedly hit the aeroplane with my machine gun fire until it struck the ground and nosed over onto its back.'

Baracca had succeeded in downing Albatros D III 153.266, which crashed in a cultivated field near San Biagio di Collalta. The ace generously shared credit for this victory with Aliperta, Baracca recalling that 'he had helped me out by continually blocking off the enemy pilot as he attempted to retreat'. The latter, Ltn von Josipovich of *Flik* 51, emerged unscathed from the wreckage of his Albatros and was immediately captured. After the war, he resumed his career in aviation, but this time as a civilian pilot. Josipovich subsequently perished in a flying accident (*Cover artwork by Mark Postlethwaite*)

First published in Great Britain in 2009 by Osprey Publishing
Midland House, West Way, Botley, Oxford, OX2 0PH
443 Park Avenue South, New York, NY, 10016, USA
E-mail; info@ospreypublishing.com

ISBN 13; 978 1 84603 426 8

Edited by Bruce Hales-Dutton and Tony Holmes
Page design by Tony Truscott
Cover Artwork by Mark Postlethwaite
Aircraft Profiles by Harry Dempsey
Scale Drawings by Mark Styling
Index by Alan Thatcher

Printed and bound in China through Bookbuilders

07 08 09 10 11 10 9 8 7 6 5 4 3 2 1

FOR A CATALOGUE OF ALL BOOKS PUBLISHED BY OSPREY MILITARY AND AVIATION PLEASE CONTACT:

Osprey Direct, c/o Random House Distribution Center,
400 Hahn Road, Westminster, MD 21157
Email: uscustomerservice@ospreypublishing.com

Osprey Direct, The Book Service Ltd, Distribution Centre,
Colchester Road, Frating Green, Colchester, Essex, CO7 7DW
E-mail: customerservice@ospreypublishing.com

www.ospreypublishing.com

CONTENTS

INTRODUCTION 6

CHAPTER ONE
ITALIAN FIGHTERS 7

CHAPTER TWO
VICTORY CLAIMS 11

CHAPTER THREE
THE ACES 13

APPENDICES 99
COLOUR PLATES COMMENTARY 99
INDEX 104

INTRODUCTION

When Italy entered the war on 24 May 1915, the *Regio Esercito* (Royal Army) was poorly equipped and lacked the modern weapons – especially machine guns and heavy artillery pieces – essential for trench warfare. Under the leadership of Gen Luigi Cadorna, Italian troops crossed the Austro-Hungarian border. In spite of the few enemy troops defending this area of the front, the Royal Army's cautious advance gave their opponents time to reinforce their positions and make the most of the high ground that they held. Minimal territory was gained, and in a short time a stalemate had been reached.

The front stabilised, assuming a shape that resembled a horizontal 'S' along the River Isonzo from the Swiss border near Trentino to the Adriatic. Almost everywhere along the frontline the terrain was mountainous. The Italian Supreme Command concentrated its efforts on the Isonzo Front, and in the Carso area the Royal Army encountered even stronger defensive works on higher ground. Thousands of men died in this area for no result.

In March 1916, following five offensives called the Battles of the Isonzo, the Italians had to face an Austro-Hungarian attack in the Northern Sector from Trentino across the Asiago Plateau. This was the *Strafexpedition* (punitive expedition), aimed at pouring forces into the Venetian plain in an effort to cut off the greater part of the Italian Army, which would then be unbalanced towards the east. Despite initially losing ground to the enemy, Italian troops were able to parry the blow and regain the offensive in the Carso area. Indeed, they were eventually able to take the city of Gorizia during the sixth Isonzo battle, only to face a new defensive line directly beyond it.

By then Gen Cadorna had become notorious for his disregard of soldiers' lives in useless frontal assaults, the complete indifference to his men's discomfort in their horrible trench life and the iron discipline that he enforced largely through firing squads. He repeated the attacks (the so called *spallate* or shoulder-blows) with few results other than to take the army to the brink of mutiny.

Despite suffering from exhaustion, Italian troops succeeded in pushing their adversaries virtually to breaking point during the 10th and 11th Isonzo battles. With Austro-Hungarian forces unable to withstand another push, their German allies came to the rescue by sending in a strong and well-equipped contingent led by the experienced Gen Otto von Below. He launched an offensive in the Upper Isonzo sector, which until then had been relatively quiet, on 24 October 1917. Although Cadorna had suspected an offensive was in the offing, several factors – including poor military leadership, low morale, new adversary tactics and the almost immediate breakdown of communication – resulted in the front being broken. The breach came near the hamlet of Caporetto (now Kobarid, in Slovenia), a name which for Italians has become synonymous with defeat.

The *Regio Esercito* retreated westwards. It was almost a rout, with the force retiring well beyond the original border and losing huge numbers of men and much material in the process. Cadorna shamefully blamed his men, accusing them of surrendering without fighting. But while some units did give up almost immediately, others fought hard and contested every step westwards. While Britain and France hurried to send reinforcements to their endangered ally, Cadorna was replaced by Gen Armando Diaz. Thanks to help from their allies, Italian troops were able to dig in along the River Piave on the Venetian plain. The invaders were halted. In the first months of 1918, while the *Regio Esercito* rebuilt its morale and strengthened its positions, the Germans withdrew from the Italian front. The Austro-Hungarian situation swiftly worsened due to critical shortages of raw materials and food, as well as to the growing tensions between the many nationalities forming the Hapsburg Empire.

In June 1918 the Austro-Hungarians launched a desperate offensive aimed at forcing Italy to sue for peace. This time the Italians were ready and did not repeat the mistakes of the previous October. Although the Austro-Hungarians crossed the Piave and established bridgeheads on the Montello Hill and near the mouth of the river, a series of Italian counterattacks, aided by British and French troops, pushed the enemy back after several days of fighting. The last Austro-Hungarian hope of winning the war had vanished. The army, like the whole empire, agonised during the summer, shaken to its core by the pangs of hunger, desperation and nationalistic demands.

On 24 October 1918, just a year after the Caporetto disaster, the Italians attacked across the Piave towards the town of Vittorio Veneto. On 3 November Austro-Hungarian plenipotentiaries signed the armistice that came into effect at 0300 hrs the following day. The conflict between Italy and the Austro-Hungarian Empire was over.

ITALIAN FIGHTERS

In the first decade of the 20th century Italy was still not fully industrialised. When war broke out in Europe, the air services of the *Regio Esercito* (Royal Army) and *Regia Marina* (Royal Navy) had few aircraft and pilots. Anticipating its entry in the war on the Allied side, Italy asked Britain and France to help meet its immediate needs by

supplying aircraft to defend its skies against enemy raids. France granted Italy a licence to build the two-seat Nieuport 10 and agreed to train pilots for these aircraft in its flying schools. After Italy declared war on Austria-Hungary, France sent a seaplane and a fighter unit to defend Venice.

The Imperial airmen were very active from the outbreak of the war. They made repeated attacks and were vainly opposed by the first Italian fighter unit, *8ª Squadriglia Nieuport*, whose efforts were hamstrung by the poor performance of the aircraft. In a desperate attempt to improve the speed and rate-of-climb of the Nieuport 10, the Italians lightened the aircraft by leaving the gunner on the ground. No enemy aircraft were downed, however. On the rare occasions when they were able to catch the raiders, the Italian pilots often found that their machine guns jammed.

Changing the unit's name to *1ª Squadriglia Caccia* (1st Fighter squadron) on 1 December 1915 did not improve matters. Summarising the situation with bitter sarcasm, Francesco Baracca, who would later become Italy's 'ace of aces', wrote in his diary, 'Scanavino wounded himself in his foot handling the Mauser – perhaps the squadron's only victim in five months of war'.

FIRST COMBAT

1ª Squadriglia Caccia shared its frustrations with *2ª Squadriglia Caccia*, which arrived at the front in January 1916. *3ª* and *4ª Squadriglia* were air defence units based in Brescia and Verona, respectively, and equipped with Italian-built Aviatiks which never encountered the enemy.

Italian and French officers gather round a Nieuport 10 trainer at Le Bourget airfield in the early summer of 1915. The tall man in civilian clothes on the right is Tenente Francesco Baracca. With him, also in civilian clothes, are Capitani Oreste Salomone and Guido Tacchini, while Capitano Maffeo Scarpis is in uniform. Salomone later transferred to a bomber unit and became the first Italian airman to receive the *Medaglia d'Oro al Valor Militare* for his gallant actions on 18 February 1916. That day, Italian Capronis attempted the first ever strategic bombing mission when they attacked Ljubljana. Salomone's aircraft was badly damaged during the course of the operation, and he nursed his crippled aircraft home with his dead comrades on board (*Fotomuseo Panini*)

Nieuport 10 383 was photographed on San Caterina airfield, near Udine. This Macchi-built machine came to *8ª Squadriglia Nieuport* on 12 September 1915, and it was among the first aircraft issued to the unit to be flown operationally by Baracca. The aircraft's poor rate-of-climb, combined with a lack of an effective air raid warning service, meant that Italian airmen serving with *8ª Squadriglia Nieuport* were usually unable to intercept enemy bombers prior to them dropping their deadly cargo and heading for home. The pilot sat in the cockpit of 383 is possibly Capitano Maffeo Scarpis (*Gianclaudio Polidori via Gregory Alegi*)

The situation improved a few months later when the new Nieuport 11 reached the front. The aircraft had a better rate-of-climb and was armed with the effective British Lewis machine gun. It was the first aircraft deployed by the Italians which really deserved to be called a fighter, and Baracca put its qualities to good use when he scored Italy's first aerial victory on 7 April 1916. This was followed almost 15 minutes later by the second, achieved by Luigi Olivari. Soon, the *Luftfahrtruppen* had lost its ability to operate with impunity. More Italian fighter units were arriving at the front and forcing a greater number of air combats.

On 15 April unit designations were standardised by the adoption of a single numeral. A *Sezione Nieuport* (Nieuport Flight) was also deployed to Albania in December to fight in that theatre. Only the Army operated specific fighter units and aircraft, while the Navy concentrated on overcoming its initial weaknesses by introducing the general purpose FBA and Macchi L flying boats. In December the Italian fighter squadrons were as follows;

Squadron	Group	Airfield
70ª (ex-*1ª Sqn Caccia*)	Autonomous	Campoformido
71ª (ex-*2ª Sqn Caccia*)	*III Gruppo*	Villaverla
72ª (ex-*3ª Sqn Caccia*)	*III Gruppo*	Brescia
73ª (ex-*4ª Sqn Caccia*)	*III Gruppo*	San Anna Alfaedo
74ª	Autonomous	Milano
75ª	*III Gruppo*	Verona
76ª	*II Gruppo*	S Maria La Longa
77ª	*I Gruppo*	Istrana

HOPES AND FEARS

In 1917 the Italian fighter force continued to grow in both numbers and strength. New aircraft from France – especially the powerful SPAD VII, the nimble Hanriot HD 1 (largely built in Italy by Macchi) and the Nieuport 27 – also helped to tip the scales further in favour of the Italians. That same year also saw the establishment of the Aerial Gunnery School, as well as several defence flights near potential targets in parts of Italy.

During the summer the *Regia Marina* began receiving early examples of the Macchi M.5 – its first flying boat designed as a fighter. Initially, the aircraft was assigned piecemeal to several units, but from November they were all delivered to two dedicated naval fighter squadrons that had been newly established in Venice.

Italian fighters took part in all the battles fought during the year, defending the skies over their territory, escorting both reconnaissance aircraft and bombers beyond the frontlines and eventually gaining air supremacy for the first time. To reverse this situation, skilled and experienced German airmen were sent to the front in October to support their troops during the 11th Isonzo battle. Due to their

An Italian Nieuport 11 is warmed up before flight. Also dubbed the *Bébé* or *Niuportino* (Little Nieuport) by the Italians, this aircraft was the first effective fighter used by the *Regio Esercito*. The arrival of the Lewis gun was also much appreciated, although the poor quality of the Italian-made ammunition led to frequent jams (*Fotomuseo Panini*)

One of the new fighter types introduced by the Italians in 1917 was the Hanriot HD 1. Nimble, easy to fly and with a good rate-of-climb, the aircraft was loved by its pilots and feared by its adversaries. A captured Austro-Hungarian pilot called it 'the fighter with V-shaped wings'. Hanriot 519, pictured here at Casoni airfield in 1918, was the personal mount of Tenente Giuseppe Retinò. His leather helmet, visible between the right strut and bracing wire, was decorated with a skull and crossbones insignia (*Francesco Ballista*)

The burned-out skeleton of a Hanriot HD 1 is pictured at an unknown airfield after being abandoned by the Italians following the Caporetto retreat. As often happens in retreats, many aircraft that needed only minor repairs were destroyed so as to prevent them falling into the hands of the enemy. *78ª Squadriglia* alone left 12 wrecked Hanriots at Borgnano (*Csirok Zoltan*)

better tactics and excellent aircraft, the Germans wrought havoc amongst the loose Italian patrols as the latter tried to slow the advancing enemy troops.

Italian fighter units did their best, but eventually they had to abandon their airfields and escape west across the River Piave. Such was the scale of the defeat that by 11 November only 220 aircraft remained to face 411 enemy machines of all types listed at the front on 24 October. Beaten, but not defeated, Italian fighter pilots took their revenge on 26 December when German aircraft attacked Istrana airfield in retaliation for the famous raid carried out against them by Royal Flying Corps ace 'Billy' Barker on Christmas Day. During the 'Istrana Air Battle', the Italians, and their British comrades, shot down at least 11 enemy aircraft without loss.

The Italian order of battle on 20 November 1917 listed the following fighter squadrons;

Squadron	Group	Airfield
70ª	*X Gruppo*	Istrana
71ª	*IX Gruppo*	Villaverla
72ª	*III Gruppo*	Verona
73ª	Autonomous	Thessaloniki (Macedonia)
75ª	*III Gruppo*	Verona
76ª	*IV Gruppo*	Istrana
77ª	*XIII Gruppo*	Marcon
78ª	*IV Gruppo*	Istrana
79ª	*VII Gruppo*	Nove and Padova
80ª	*XIII Gruppo*	Marcon
81ª	*IV Gruppo*	Istrana
82ª	*X Gruppo*	Istrana
83ª (Second Flight)	*XIII Gruppo*	Marcon
84ª	*XIII Gruppo*	Marcon
91ª	*X Gruppo*	Padova
260ª	-	Venice
261ª	-	Venice (being formed)

FINAL VICTORY

Taking advantage of the lull imposed by winter, the Italian squadrons used the first months of 1918 to regain their strength and train in the new air tactics introduced the previous October by the Germans. The *Regia Marina* also increased the size of its fighter units.

Under the control of the newly formed *Ispettorato delle Squadriglie da Caccia* (Inspectorate of Fighter Squadrons), led by Tenente Colonnello Pier Ruggero Piccio – an ace with outstanding leadership skills – Army fighter pilots learned to fly in formation, with clearly defined patrol discipline and individual roles. Piccio also codified the first Italian rules for the employment of fighters in combat. They were issued as the *Istruzione provvisoria di impiego delle Squadriglie da Caccia*

(Provisional Instruction for the use of the Fighter Squadrons). The content of this document displayed a clear understanding of air combat, and is to some extent still valid today.

The hard training was used to advantage in June when the Austro-Hungarians made their last, ill-fated, attempt to win the war. The action of the Italian fighters, gathered in a mass to operate jointly where required, was a key factor in the victory. From the first day of the attack, on 15 June, the Italian fighters wiped the enemy aircraft from the sky, inflicting such losses on the *Luftfahrtruppen* that this period came to be known as the *Schwarzwochen* (Black Weeks). Having gained air supremacy, and with *drachen*, bombers and reconnaissance aircraft free to perform their duties, Italian fighters strafed troops and dropped small bombs in a way that foreshadowed the close air support missions flown in World War 2. The same happened in October when Italy administered the *coup de grace* to the collapsing Hapsburg empire.

Hastily conceived at the outbreak of war, the Italian fighter force had become a powerful and flexible weapon, well equipped and well-manned.

These fighter units featured in the order of battle on 4 November 1918;

Top
The sad end of Albatros D III 153.266, shot down on 15 June 1918, seems to symbolise the state of the *Luftfährtruppe* after the last offensive. According to an Austrian source, the *Isonzoarmee* lost 22 per cent of its pilots, 19 per cent of its observers and 41 per cent of its aircraft between 15 and 24 June 1918. The Austro-Hungarian air force never recovered its strength

Above
The stripped wrecks of a handful of Albatros D IIIs are seen here after having been lined up by the Italians on Bressanone airfield on a cold November day in 1918. After the war the Italians tested many German and Austro-Hungarian types at Montecelio airfield, now Guidonia, near Rome, before scrapping them

Squadron	Group	Airfield
70ᵃ	X Gruppo	Gazzo
71ᵃ	XVII Gruppo	Quinto di Treviso
72ᵃ	XVII Gruppo	Quinto di Treviso
73ᵃ	XXI Gruppo	Thessaloniki (Macedonia)
74ᵃ	XX Gruppo	Ponte San Marco
75ᵃ	III Gruppo	Ganfardine
76ᵃ	IV Gruppo	Casoni
77ᵃ	XVII Gruppo	Marcon
78ᵃ	XXIII Gruppo	San Luca
79ᵃ	XXIII Gruppo	San Luca
80ᵃ	XIII Gruppo	Marcon
81ᵃ	IV Gruppo	Casoni
82ᵃ	X Gruppo	Gazzo
83ᵃ	XXIV Gruppo	Poianella
85ᵃ	VIII Gruppo	Valona (Albania)
91ᵃ	XVII Gruppo	Quinto di Treviso
260ᵃ	Gruppo Idrocaccia Venezia	Venice
261ᵃ	Gruppo Idrocaccia Venezia	Venice
262ᵃ	–	Brindisi

VICTORY CLAIMS

During World War 1, the *Entente* countries standardised the term 'Ace' to recognise a pilot who had shot down at least five enemy aircraft, but every service had its own rules for the confirmation or denial of a claim. The first known official Italian victory validation criteria can be dated to late 1918, but even without explicit documentation the method previously followed is easily reconstructed.

Although the criteria adopted during the first period of the war differed slightly between units, generally speaking the rules were very strict and rigorously followed. With the logical exception of enemy aircraft falling in their own territory, a victory was confirmed only when there were independent confirmations from other pilots or ground observers, who attested that the opponent had been destroyed in a crash or had burned. In exceptional cases, if the pilot's veracity had been proved, a victory could be confirmed even without witnesses. This happened very rarely.

Confirmation could also come from other sources, including intelligence, interrogation of prisoners, deserters or Italian soldiers who had escaped from captivity. This meant that often a claim would receive homologation several months later. For instance Baracca's third victory, scored on 23 August 1916, was confirmed only in April 1917. A victory could be also shared among several pilots, with each of them receiving full credit, but this seems to have depended on the specific circumstances of the fight and the different roles the pilots played in it.

To further standardise these procedures, the 'Provisional Instruction for the use of the Fighter Squadrons', issued in June 1918, by Tenente Colonnello Piccio, codified the system for the first time. The document stated that homologating a victory required 'at least' two certain confirmations from artillery, kite-balloon or frontline observers. Lacking such verification, victories could be validated only in exceptional cases when the destruction of the enemy aircraft was confirmed by the unanimous reports of other pilots or statements from prisoners.

In January 1919 the intelligence branch of the *Comando Generale di Aeronautica* (General Command of Aeronautics) re-examined all Italian victory claims and drew up the official list of the Italian Army airmen that

This photograph of Nieuport scouts from *70ª Squadriglia* includes Br C I 61.57 of *Flik* 19, which was forced down by Baracca on 7 April 1916 near Medeuzza for his first victory, and also the first for the Italian air force. The machine was repaired at the Aviano workshop and then flown to Santa Caterina by Baracca himself. Displaying large Italian markings, the Br CI was briefly used by its new owners to improve the aircraft recognition skills of Italian anti-aircraft gunners. The Br C I was eventually destroyed by Italian troops so as to prevent it falling into the hands of its former owners when Caterina airfield was abandoned to the Austro-Hungarians in October 1917 (*Fotomuseo Panini*)

The table of Italian *Regio Esercito* aces published by the aviation magazine *Il Cielo* on 25 March 1919. Portraits of Bedendo, Masiero and Riva were not available at the time, which meant that they had to be replaced by sketches of flying helmets. Pilots whose portraits were outlined in black had not survived the war

had shot down at least one enemy aeroplane. It also sent each airman a letter explaining what was confirmed and what was not. Despite much scouring of archives, the author has failed to locate documentation explaining the criteria followed in the review. However, having studied Italian sources, and those of their former allies and enemies, it appears to the author that the re-evaluation carried out in 1919 confirmed that most of the victories claimed during the war tallied with actual enemy losses. Despite this, it should also be remembered that archives in Italy, Austria and other countries involved in the conflict are not complete, and a number of victories, therefore, remain uncorroborated by official documentation.

Notice to the reader

Compiling the lists of the victories obtained by an ace for this volume, as for his previous works, the author had to identify the victories officially confirmed after the war (only a handful of the original letters issued by the intelligence branch seem to have survived) and then to try to match claims with possible victims. Not every 'confirmed victory' has its corresponding actual loss, and vice-versa. Some combats are confirmed, others almost certainly took place, but the great majority of them are subject to varying degrees of uncertainty. The reader will therefore find under the 'Victory' heading the list of victories officially confirmed after the war, while under the heading 'Victim' we have listed, wherever possible, the actual or possible opponent of the Italian pilot in that fight. Due to further research, in some cases the lists differ slightly from those published by the same author in his previous books.

THE ACES

Michele Allasia

Born in Ferrara on 20 June 1895, Michele Allasia was just 18 years old when, in 1913, he was accepted by the *Battaglione Squadriglie Aviatori*, (the heavier-than-air branch of the Italian Army air service) because of his civilian occupation of lathe operator. After the outbreak of war, Allasia was enrolled in the flying school and obtained his licence on 22 May 1916. His first assignment was to *37ª Squadriglia*, which was a Farman unit charged with defending Bergamo. In November, after 40 uneventful patrols, Allasia was selected for Nieuport training and eventually returned to the Isonzo Front, where he was assigned to *80ª Squadriglia*. He was immediately engaged in escort missions over enemy territory. On 27 April the young sergente maggiore wrote to his family;

'Yesterday I had a very hard air combat. I was escorting a Caproni at an altitude of 4600 m (15,000 ft) when, near Trieste, I saw three Austro-Hungarian aeroplanes that quickly attacked us. I immediately faced the adversaries so to allow the Caproni to escape. I was surrounded and pounded by hits, but eventually gained an additional 100 m (325 ft) of height after what seemed like a thousand aerobatics. In this way I was able to get away. If only you could see how badly holed my aircraft is! Four bullets grazed my back. Even the fuel tank was pierced.'

At around this time the 'Happy Hooligan' cartoon character, well known to Italians as *Fortunello* ('Lucky Man'), appeared on the fuselage of *80ª Squadriglia's* Nieuport 11s as its insignia. Several versions were applied to the aircraft, as Allasia noted in another letter home;

'The son of *Fortunello* who laughs is painted on my aircraft. I hope that it will bring me good luck.'

Perhaps the luck only held good in combat with enemy aircraft for on 10 May Allasia was wounded by a splinter from an anti-aircraft shell and forced to land near Doberdò. Hospitalised, he did not return to his unit until July. On 10 August Allasia scored his first victory when he and Tenente Sabelli shared in the destruction of a Br C I which was seen 'burning and falling in the vicinity of Mount Stol'.

In November, after the Caporetto retreat, Allasia, now an aspirante ufficiale, was transferred to *77ª Squadriglia* in Marcon, where he began flying the SPAD VII.

On 11 March 1918, having by now been promoted to sottotenente, Allasia flew his scout across the River Piave on a reconnaissance mission over Pordenone, where he was engaged by a formation of Austrian-Hungarian fighters. Somehow he was able to return home safely, despite his SPAD having been hit 18 times by rounds

Michele Allasia poses atop his Macchi-built Nieuport 11 in the spring of 1917. Although he wrote in a letter that he had chosen as his insignia 'a laughing "Happy Hooligan"', its face suggests a more menacing expression toward the enemy. The uniformed officer standing immediately right of the cockpit is Alessandro Resch of reconnaissance unit *25ª Squadriglia*. He subsequently became an ace in July 1918 (*Roberto Gentilli*)

fired by 28-victory ace Fiala von Fernbrugg, who claimed to have shot down a 'Sopwith' near Spresiano. On 8 June 1918 Allasia was transferred to newly-formed strategic reconnaissance unit *5ª Sezione SVA* at Fossalunga. However, on 20 July his two-seat SVA 9 (11712) crashed near Marcon airfield and caught fire before Allasia and his passenger, Capitano Giuseppe Graglia, could escape the wreckage.

Michele Allasia's main awards – three Silver and one Bronze Medals for Military Valour

Michele Allasia's victories

Victory	Date	Location	Victim	Notes
1	10/8/17	Monte Stol	Br C I 229.25 – *FlG* 1	With Sabelli
2	2/11/17	Codroipo	Unknown aircraft	
3	7/11/17	Livenza	German aeroplane – *FA A Abt*	
			Zgsf Friedrich Schieg	
			Oblt Friedrich Werth	
4	15/6/18	Fontigo	Unknown two-seater	
5	23/6/18	Falzè	Unknown aircraft	

Antonio Amantea is seen here with his SPAD VII – a type that he flew from December 1917 until war's end, during which time he scored two of his five confirmed victories. According to some sources, he had painted mocking words on the fighter's fuselage to taunt his opponents, but no illustrations have so far come to light to confirm this (*Roberto Gentilli*)

Antonio Amantea

Born on 28 September 1894 in Lecce, in southern Italy, Antonio Amantea worked as an electrician and volunteered for the aviation service after being drafted in September 1914. Earning his wings on 1 September 1915, Sergente Amantea was then assigned to artillery spotting unit *3ª Squadriglia Aeroplani*, equipped with Caudron G 3s, on the Isonzo Front. In February 1917, after 173 flights, Amantea was selected for fighter training, and in late March he returned to the front with *71ª Squadriglia* – a unit operating over the Asiago Plateau in the northern sector.

Amantea had to wait until 2 August to score his first confirmed victory, which took the form of an unidentified two-seater that he intercepted near Arsiero. Forced to break off his attack due to magneto failure, Amantea had to make a crash-landing. His engine ran perfectly on the 24th, however, when he attacked the Albatros D III of Fw Kowalczic, who was forced to crash-land his burning aircraft. Exactly a month later, on 24 September, Amantea again forced a D III to crash-land near Monte Pau. Its pilot, Kpl Früwirth, escaped unhurt.

In December Amantea was promoted to aspirante ufficiale and began flying the SPAD VII. He claimed his first victory of 1918 with the new fighter on 22 March when he attacked an Aviatik D I (possibly 38.16 of *Flik* 23) over Vallarsa but was unable to see it crash due to trouble with his Hispano-Suiza engine. The claim was confirmed under the strict Italian rules, however, despite the loss of his possible victim (Aviatik D I 38.16) to anti-aircraft fire according to Austrian sources. Between then and the end of the war, Amantea would score only one more victory, on 3 May.

Leaving the air service with the rank of tenente, Amantea was back in uniform by 1922. As a member of the new *Regia Aeronautica*, he would participate in the Ethiopian War and attain the rank of colonnello when

Italy entered World War 2 in June 1940. When the Italian armistice was announced on 8 September 1943, Amantea was commanding Galatina airfield. He retired in 1946 and died in Lecce on 13 August 1983.

Antonio Amantea's main awards – three Silver Medals for Military Valour

Antonio Amantea's victories

Victory	Date	Location	Victim	Notes
1	2/8/17	Arsiero	Unknown two-seater	
2	24/8/17	Luserna	Albatros D III 53.33 – *Flik* 24	
3	24/9/17	Monte Verena	Albatros D III 53.51 – *Flik* 48/D	
4	22/3/18	Vallarsa	Aviatik D I 38.16 – *Flik* 23	
5	3/5/18	Spitz	Unknown aircraft	

Giovanni Ancillotto

Although christened Giovanni, Ancillotto went by the nicknames of 'Giannino' and 'Nane'. Born into a wealthy family on 18 December 1896 in San Donà di Piave, he studied engineering in the *Politecnico di Torino* and volunteered for the air service in November 1915.

Soldato Ancillotto flew his first missions in June 1916 as a reconnaissance pilot. On 13 April 1917, now an aspirante, he left the front for fighter training, returning in June to *80ª Squadriglia* as a sottotenente. Despite flying up to two sorties a day, he was unable to score any victories until 26 October, when in two days during the Italian retreat he managed to shoot down three seaplanes that were bombing Italian infantry. After scoring another victory, on 3 November, over a German aircraft, Ancillotto was transferred to *77ª Squadriglia*, where he began flying the SPAD VII.

It was during this period that Ancillotto embarked on his career as a 'balloon-buster'. For this task he preferred the Nieuport 11, which could be equipped with Le Prieur rockets. On 30 November 1917 he set a balloon ablaze near Fossalta to score his fifth victory, followed by a second on 3 December near San Polo di Piave. The destruction of a third kite balloon 48 hours later would be an altogether more dramatic event. Finding a *Drachen* near Rustigné, Ancillotto dived on it with such enthusiasm that he had to fly through a fireball of flaming hydrogen as it erupted. He emerged on the other side with large fragments of the envelope wrapped around his fighter. This feat earned him the *Medaglia d'Oro al Valor Militare* (Gold Medal for Military Valour), which was the highest Italian award for gallantry, and prominence on the cover of the *Domenica del Corriere*, which was the most important Italian magazine at the time. Ancillotto was also dubbed the *l'ala incombusta* ('the unburned wing') by Gabriele D'Annunzio, then Italy's most famous aviator.

Unconcerned by his sudden celebrity, Ancillotto continued to fly

'Nane' Ancillotto stands up in the cockpit of his Italian-built Nieuport 17 3592 for the benefit of the camera at Aiello airfield in October 1917. He scored his first victory in this aircraft on 26 October 1917, but one month later, on 30 November, switched back to a Nieuport 11 when instructed to attack a *Drachen* balloon because the older fighter could be equipped with Le Prieur rockets – the perfect weapon for 'balloon-busting'. Although it lacked an explosive or incendiary charge, the rocket could set fire to the balloon with its flaming trail. Nieuport 17 3592 survived the October retreat and was subsequently used as pilot trainer the following spring (*Fotomuseo Panini*)

'Balloon-buster' 'Nane' Ancillotto poses with his Nieuport 11 at Marcon shortly after flaming a *Drachen* at Rustigné on 5 December 1917. The veteran scout is liberally covered with large fragments of fabric from the balloon's gas bag. The tubes carrying the Le Prieur rockets are mounted on the wing struts, and at least one weapon is apparently still in its mounting on the left-hand side. Part of the fabric was used to make a raincoat for the Duke of Aosta, commander of the Italian III Army to which *77ª Squadriglia* was subordinated! (*Roberto Gentilli*)

missions and began to consider how to counter the new threat posed by night raids. With his usual dash, he committed himself to the task of flying at night after his habitual diurnal operations. On the night of 24 July Ancillotto finally scored a nocturnal victory while flying a Hanriot HD 1. He wrote in his combat report;

'I scrambled at 0035 hrs and cruised over the airfield for some time until I saw an enemy aeroplane caught by the beam of a searchlight. Immediately, I came towards it and reached it in a few seconds. I fired a burst, sending it crashing near Trepalade. When coming back to land after the first fight I saw tracers over Casale. Suddenly, I was able to sight another enemy aeroplane and pursued it at once, firing a strong burst. I managed to knock down the second aeroplane near Sant'Elena sul Sile.'

Ancillotto shared his last victory on 27 October 1918 with Capitano Filippo Serafini. Spotting a fighter chasing a British Sopwith Camel, they rushed to help their ally. Although they arrived too late to save Lt G A Goodman of No 66 Sqn, who perished in E1579, they did down his opponent. By war's end Ancillotto had logged 315 operational flights.

Post-war, he flew to Poland in an SVA, accompanied Gabriele D'Annunzio to Fiume, in the Balkans, flew over the Andes in Peru and visited Somalia. On 17 October 1924 Ancillotto was driving from Turin to his birthplace when he crashed in Caravaggio and was killed.

Giovanni Ancillotto's main awards – one Gold and three Silver Medals for Military Valour

Giovanni Ancillotto's victories

Victory	Date	Location	Victim	Notes
1	26/10/17	Brestovica	K367 seaplane, Frwg Tröber and Ltn Obendorfer both unhurt	
2	26/10/17	Doberdò Lake	K212 seaplane, Frg Ltn M Kramer von Drauberg died of wounds and Flgmr Marcello Anasipoli PoW	With Cabruna, Leonardi & Lombardi
3	27/10/17	Doberdò Lake	K366 seaplane	
4	3/11/17	Rovarè	DFW C V – unit unknown	
5	30/11/17	Fossalta	*Drachen – BK* 13	
6	3/12/17	San Polo	*Drachen – BK* 10	
7	5/12/17	Rustigné	*Drachen – BK* 2	
8	24/7/18	Sile	Br C I 129.38 – *Flik* 101/G	
9	24/7/18	San Elena	Br C I 169.161 – *Flik* 101/G	
10	21/8/18	Ponte di Piave	Br C I 369.143 – *Flik* 19/D, pilot unknown and unhurt	
11	27/10/18	San Fior	Unknown fighter	With Serafini & several British pilots

Flaminio Avet

Count Flaminio Avet was born in Bendejun, near Nice, on 3 August 1890 into a noble family. He completed his law studies in Rome in 1914, but soon left the courts for the saddle as a member of the *Lancieri di Firenze* Regiment. Like many other cavalrymen, Avet was transferred to a more modern branch of the military – he was transferred to the 37th Field Artillery Regiment on the rocky Carso hills in August 1915. His courage in directing fire on 25 November 1915 in spite of heavy enemy shelling brought him his first *Medaglia d'Argento al Valor Militare.*

After applying for a transfer to aviation, Avet was admitted to flying school in May 1916 and eventually assigned to *73ª Squadriglia* (a reconnaissance unit based at Verona) on 3 February 1917. At the end of August 1917 he left Verona for fighter conversion training, returning to the front just in time to become embroiled in the disastrous 12th Isonzo battle.

Assigned to *82ª Squadriglia,* Avet had a close shave on the cloudy morning of 26 December when German aircraft attacked his airfield just as he was taxying out in his Hanriot. With his scout riddled with bullets, Avet jumped into another fighter and took off in pursuit of the enemy. Despite encountering numerous German aircraft during the ensuing air battle, Avet failed to register a victory.

In January 1918 he moved from *82ª Squadriglia* to *70ª Squadriglia,* with whom he finally claimed his first victories on 17 April 1918 – he credited with successes on this date. Avet and his patrol were cruising over the River Piave, flying from Ponte della Priula to Quero, when they sighted an Austro-Hungarian Br C I escorted by Albatros D IIIs. Unseen by the enemy, Avet led his wingmen into a favourable position prior to diving on the enemy formation. The first to fall to the hail of Vickers bullets was Albatros 153.152, followed by C I 169.35, which went down in spite of the desperate action of the escorting fighters. Both Italian claims match Austrian losses, while the third victory could be the Albatros of Oblt Fitz, who coaxed his badly damaged scout home.

Avet's next victory came on 3 May when he and his patrol encountered *Flik* 63/J. The latter unit lost its squadron commander, Oblt Josef Lederer, during the dogfight, and then saw two more of its Phönix D I fighters fall to the Camels of No 66 Sqn minutes later.

On 17 May Avet became an ace when he shot down a Br C I near Maserada, then, on 15 July, during yet another patrol over the Piave, he claimed two more enemy fighters destroyed. Although confirmed by the strict Italian rules, these claims do not match any known Austrian losses. Avet's last confirmed victory came on 28 October without him having to fire a single shot. Flying with his usual wingmen Eleuteri and Bocchese, he suffered jammed guns, but the crew of the opposing Aviatik D I chose to surrender and landed near Arcade. Avet ended the

Count Flaminio Avet and his war-weary Hanriot HD 1 in late 1918. This French-built machine was in use from the spring of that year, and during its long operational career its nose panels were replaced by Italian-made components. Barely visible in front of the windscreen is an unusual ring-and-bead sight. The tricolour patches on the uppersurfaces of the top wing cover splinter damage inflicted on 18 March 1918 (*Avet family*)

war as CO of *70ª Squadriglia* with 200+ combat missions to his credit. He returned to civilian life, married and had a daughter, but his health prematurely deteriorated and he died in Bendejun on 21 August 1928.

Flaminio Avet's main awards – two Silver Medals for Military Valour

Flaminio Avet's victories

Victory	Date	Location	Victim	Notes
1	17/4/18	Valdobbiadene	Br C I 169.35 – *Flik* 52/D	With Bocchese & Eleuteri
2	17/4/18	Valdobbiadene	Albatros D III 153.152 – *Flik* 42/J	With Bocchese & Eleuteri
3	17/4/18	Valdobbiadene	Albatros D III unknown – *Flik* 42/J	With Bocchese & Eleuteri
4	3/5/18	Zenson	Phönix D I 228.42 – *Flik* 63/J	
5	17/5/18	Maserada	Br C I 229.30 – *Flik* 124/Rb	
6	15/7/18	Vidor	Aviatik D I 38.63 – *Flik* 74/J	With Bocchese & Eleuteri
7	15/7/18	Sernaglia	Unknown fighter	With Bocchese & Eleuteri
8	28/10/18	Arcade	Aviatik D I unknown	With Bocchese & Eleuteri

Francesco Baracca

The life of the man who was to become Italy's 'ace of aces' in World War 1 – and the first to display a symbol which, thanks to Enzo Ferrari, is still famous around the world today – began on 8 May 1888 in the small town of Lugo, near Ravenna. The only son of a wealthy landowner, Baracca was sent to a private school near Florence after completing primary studies in his home town. He found relief from the boredom of the classroom in horse riding, which was a passion that was to stay with him for the whole of his life. After high school he volunteered for the Military Academy.

In 1910 Sottotenente Baracca went to Rome to join the prestigious *Piemonte Reale Cavalleria*, a cavalry regiment with origins in the 17th century. In the capital the young officer distinguished himself not only through the performance of his duties but also in his enjoyment of society's 'delights' – particularly hunting and going to concerts and the opera. He also gained fame through participation in equestrian competitions. This *dolce vita* was interrupted by a period of service in a small town in central Italy, however, and Baracca, possibly seeking to add some spice to his life of routine, volunteered for the flying service. Coming to aviation by chance, as he would later confess in a letter, Baracca immediately fell in love with it. After obtaining his pilot's licence in Reims, France, on 9 July 1912, Baracca returned to Italy and toured several airfields and units.

When war broke out in Europe, neutral Italy soon saw its political climate become red-hot following a series of disputes between war and peace parties. Baracca maintained a

On 7 April 1916 Baracca scored not only his first aerial victory but also the first for the Italian air force. On that day he was flying this French-built Nieuport 11 (1451), which he regularly patrolled in between March and October 1916, when *70ª Squadriglia* received its first Nieuport 17s. Long-lived 1451 was last recorded as being in operation in March 1918, when it was used by *110ª Squadriglia* in the defence of Naples (*Fotomuseo Panini*)

neutral attitude, ready to do his duty with a solid patriotism that differed from the interventionist fury displayed by many others. His skill as an aviator had already been noticed, and his name was added to the list of the most competent Italian pilots who were duly sent to France for fighter training at Le Bourget once Italy entered the war on the Allied side. When he returned, in July 1915, Baracca was assigned to *8ᵃ Squadriglia Nieuport*. Due to frequent gun jamming and the poor performance of its Nieuport 10s, *8ᵃ Squadriglia Nieuport* got off to a disappointing start. Things quickly improved when the first Lewis-equipped Nieuport 11s arrived.

Br C I 61.57 is seen here at an Italian airfield, probably Medeuzza, immediately after its capture on 7 April 1916. The aircraft was forced to land with a holed fuel tank, and its pilot, Fw Adolf Ott, was unable to set it alight before the arrival of Italian soldiers. He had been trying to help his wounded observer, Oblt Franz Lenarcic, who would later die. The 'Albatros', as the Italians called it, briefly flew in Italian colours before being taken to Mirafiori, near Turin, for further flight testing (*Mauro Antonellini*)

On 7 April 1916 Baracca scrambled from San Caterina airfield and engaged a Br C I of *Flik* 19. Having holed the two-seater's fuel tank, Baracca forced it to land in a field near Medeuzza. Aside from being his first victory, it was also the first for the Italian air force. This success highlighted some of the traits that would characterise Baracca both as a fighter pilot and a human being. He liked to manoeuvre his aircraft into the enemy's blind spot, behind and below him, and then fire a long burst at point-blank range. The unjacketed bullets then in use destroyed machines and caused terrible injuries to their crews. Baracca was well aware of this, and although he did not shirk from his duty in the air, he always showed respect for his victims by visiting the wounded in hospital or placing wreaths on the graves of these he had killed.

The airman's fame grew with his victory list, and Baracca soon became a national hero, acclaimed by colleagues and senior officers as well as by the press. By 1 May 1917, when the best Italian fighter pilots (including Baracca) were brought together to man the new *91ᵃ Squadriglia*, his score stood at nine victories.

It was during this period that the soon-to-be-famous black prancing horse first appeared on the fuselage of his Nieuport 17. It has been suggested that Baracca adopted it after shooting down a pilot from the German city of Stuttgart, whose crest features a prancing horse. This cannot be true, however, as German aviation units did not arrive in Italy until October 1917. Baracca himself explained the insignia's real origin in one of his many letters, stating that he chose the prancing horse as a tribute to *Piemonte Reale Cavalleria*, whose crest featured the device in silver on a red background.

At first Baracca was able to avoid being appointed squadron commander of the new unit, but he was eventually obliged to accept the role with its responsibility and much-despised paperwork. Yet he was still able to continue flying, and to score victories, often accompanied by his friends Ruffo and Piccio. On 22 October he also became the first Italian pilot to shoot down a German aircraft (a DFW C V). After the rout at Caporetto, Baracca reorganised *91ᵃ Squadriglia* and, fully aware of the importance of morale as well as equipment, he promoted the adoption of a squadron insignia that could be displayed on the unit's SPAD VIIs, together with

The soon to be famous black prancing horse first appeared on Nieuport 17 2614 at some point between January and May 1917 – it was displayed on both sides of the fuselage. At the time Baracca was gathering the best Italian fighter pilots within *91ª Squadriglia*, which was soon dubbed *La Squadriglia degli Assi* ('The Aces Squadron'). Baracca, keen on horses and the winner of various equestrian competitions pre-war, chose the insignia in honour of his cavalry regiment, *Piemonte Reale Cavalleria*, whose crest consisted of a silver horse on a red field

The prancing horse later adorned the SPAD VIIs assigned to *91ª Squadriglia*. Italian pilots liked this fighter because of its power and strength, but they encountered many problems with the Italian-built engines fitted to the aircraft, leading pilots to acquire French-made ones for their scouts. The wrap-around windscreen seen here was also disliked by pilots, who preferred the smaller one which let less wind into the cockpit (*Maurizio Longoni*)

personal markings to generate an *espirit de corps*. The unit's griffon insignia was, however, not added to the aircraft until the spring of 1918.

Promoted to *maggiore* in recognition of his success, Baracca was awarded the *Medaglia d'Oro al Valor Militare* on 25 March 1918. The highest Italian gallantry decoration was seldom awarded to living soldiers.

Baracca, who had not scored since 7 December 1917, achieved his first victory of 1918 on 3 May over a Br C I, as he wrote in his combat report;

'I saw it being attacked by Sergente Nardini who, after firing about 20 rounds, was forced to abandon the fight due to his gun jamming. I came down and attacked the "Albatros" over enemy lines at about 3200 m (10,400 ft). After my first volley it descended in a spiral for 1000 m (3250 ft) and then resumed flying towards our lines. I attacked a second time from below and from the side, then again from behind in a third attack until the enemy aircraft was clearly on fire. It crashed north of Salettuol on the banks of the Piave ahead of our lines.'

Air activity increased as the Austro-Hungarians prepared their last offensive. Baracca scored again on 22 May and then attained his last two victories on 15 June when the attack began. Flying over the lines with Sergente Aliperta as wingman, he was able to see enemy aircraft bombing Italian positions through the smoke and haze. Baracca attacked a Br C I, sending it crashing in flames near Saletto. He then spotted fighters above the two-seaters, and by diving towards Treviso, he gave them the impression that the Italian scouts were fleeing the area. Once at a safe distance, however, both the SPAD pilots gained altitude and returned. Noticing that one of the enemy Albatros D IIIs was lagging slightly behind the others, Baracca attacked it immediately. He was joined by Aliperta, and the Albatros overturned while trying to land near San Biagio di Collalta.

The Italians soon gained air supremacy, and their fighters began to strafe the Austro-Hungarian troops. These missions, flown at tree-top height and code-named *Reptile* by the Italians, meant that fighter pilots were exposed to a deadly barrage of anti-aircraft fire. The result was a veritable curtain of lead thrown up not only by artillery and machine guns but also by rifles. Well aware of the risks, Baracca was determined to face them with his usual calm and courage. This was certainly not the result of any feeling of invulnerability, but because of his respect for duty and moral integrity. Like many others, Baracca never showed his fears, hiding them behind a faint smile – just as he did on the evening of 17 June.

Returning from a strafing raid, he noticed a bullet hole in the headrest of his aircraft. It had missed him only because he had been leaning forward to aim through the fighter's Chretien gunsight.

Forty-eight hours later, Baracca chose as his wingman novice pilot Tenente Franco Osnago, who he was keen to introduce to operations at a time when enemy aircraft were unlikely to be encountered. He took off in his SPAD VII, 5382. Above

Montello, Baracca left Osnago to provide him with top cover as he dived on the enemy trenches. Watching from above, Osnago lost sight of his leader, who was obscured by the SPAD's wing. When he looked again he saw something burning among the trees in a nearby valley. Osnago saw nothing else, and returned broken-hearted to the airfield, where he delivered his report through tears. The fact that he had not seen another aircraft in the sky led his squadronmates to conclude that Baracca had been downed by enemy ground fire, and this became the official cause of his loss.

It should, however, be noted that Ltn Arnold Barwig in Phönix C I 121.17, piloted by Zgsf Max Kauer, claimed to have shot down the ace. For a while the Italians hoped that Baracca might have been taken prisoner, but on 24 June Osnago and Ranza, along with journalist Garinei, found his body. Baracca's remains were buried in his native Lugo after a funeral attended by a large crowd.

Unlike other heroes who deserved similar glory, Baracca's name was not confined to the pages of history books or to a street name. While the prancing horse continues to 'gallop' both on Ferrari sportscars and the fighters of the Italian Air Force's IX and X Groups, the name of Baracca lives on as an example – albeit one sometimes tinged with myth – of

Francesco Baracca and Fulco Ruffo di Calabria pose for a photograph taken at Aviano airfield during a ceremony in August 1917. The airmen were close friends on the ground as well as in the air, and they shared three victories. On one occasion in June 1917, Ruffo came out of the clouds firing on an enemy aircraft heading directly for him, and almost shot Baracca down in the process. Once back on the ground Baracca told Ruffo with a smile, 'Dear Fulco, next time, if you want to shoot me down, aim a couple of metres to the right. Now let's go for a drink and not talk about it anymore'! (*Mauro Antonellini*)

Baracca at Padua airfield in April 1918. Other photographs from this period show the ace wearing a more practical jacket that displayed just one ribbon (probably that of the Gold Medal), as well as puttees rather than leather boots. For this official portrait the ace is wearing a well-tailored uniform, with all his medal ribbons, and high boots with spurs. He is also holding a shooting stick. The SPAD XIII behind him has been adorned with a black horse insignia painted onto a white field. The presence of the griffon insignia on the right-hand side of the fighter's fuselage remains unconfirmed. The aircraft's serial number is also unknown, although it might be S2445. The fighter was delivered to *91ª Squadriglia* on 14 February 1918 and eventually transferred to a maintenance depot on 21 May (*Museo Francesco Baracca*)

extraordinary courage, skill and dedication, as well as of warm humanity. Almost 90 years after his death, Francesco Baracca is perhaps the only figure from World War 1 still familiar to the average Italian.

Francesco Baracca's main awards – *Ordine Militare di Savoia*, one Gold, two Silver and one Bronze Medals for Military Valour

Francesco Baracca's victories

Victory	Date	Location	Victim	Notes
1	7/4/16	Medeuzza	Br C I 61.57 – *Flik* 19	
2	16/5/16	Gorizia	Lohner 17.42 – *Flik* 12	
3	23/8/16	Merna	Br C I 61.61 – *Flik* 19	With Ruffo
4	16/9/16	Caporetto	Lloyd 43.74 – *Flik* 16	With Ruffo
5	25/11/16	Tolmezzo	Br C I 68.03 – *Flik* 16	
6	1/1/17	Castagnevizza	Br C I – *Flik* 12	
7	11/2/17	Orzano	Br C I 27.74 – *Flik* 35	With Ruffo
8	26/4/17	Gradisca	Br C I 129.17 – *Flik* 35	With Imolesi
9	1/5/17	Latisana	Br C I 229.08 – *Flik* 12	
10	10/5/17	Vertoiba	Br C I 28.17 unknown	
11	13/5/17	Monte Korada	Br C I 129.20 – *FIG* 1, Fw Julius Busa and Oblt Hermann Grössler both KIA	
12	20/5/17	Plava	Either Br C I 229.10 – *Flik* 12, Zgsf Ludwig Ferschl and Ltn d R Eugen Csutka both KIA, or Br C I 129.52 – *Flik* 12, Kpl Michael Scholz and Oblt Ludwig Varga both KIA	
13	3/6/17	NE di Plava	Br C I 129.51 – *FIG* 1	
14	7/7/17	Castagnevizza	Br C I 129.68 – *Flik* 46	
15	31/7/17	Podgora	Br C I 69.93 – *Flik* 46	
16	3/8/17	Val di Sava	Unknown aircraft	
17	19/8/17	NE di Selo	Br C I – *Flik* 28	
18	1/9/17	Zagorje	Br C I 69.10 – *FIG* 101	
19	6/9/17	San Gabriele	Br C I 129.50 – *Flik* 34	
20	22/10/17	Sabotino	DFW C V – *FA* 14, Lt d R Werner Zimmermann and Lt d R Artur Fischer both KIA	
21	22/10/17	Volnik	DFW C V – *FA* 14, Lt d R Ludwig Güttler and Ltn Heinrich Hansberg both KIA	
22	25/10/17	San Marco	Unknown aircraft	
23	26/10/17	San Lucia di Tolmino	German DFW C V – impossible to identify	With Parvis
24	26/10/17	Matajur	German DFW C V – impossible to identify	With Parvis
25	6/11/17	Fossalta	Albatros D III 153.54 – *Flik* 41	With Parvis
26	6/11/17	Godega	DFW C V – *FA (A)* 219, Vfw Werner Schröder and Ltn Albrecht Binder both KIA	With Parvis
27	7/11/17	Orsago	DFW C V 3955.17 – *FA (A)* 204, Gefr Wilhelm Appelt and Ltn Paul Wilkening both KIA	With Parvis
28	15/11/17	Istrana	DFW C V – *FA* 14	
29	23/11/17	Falzè	Albatros D III – *Jasta* 39	With Novelli
30	7/12/17	Kaberlaba	Br C I 29.20 – *Flik* 19	
31	3/5/18	Salettuol	Br C I 369.28 – *Flik* 19	
32	22/5/18	Cimadolmo	Albatros D III 153.155 – *Flik* 51	
33	15/6/18	Saletto	Br C I 369.116 – *Flik* 32/D	
34	15/6/18	San Biagio di Collalta	Albatros D III 153.266 – *Flik* 51	With Aliperta

Flavio Torello Baracchini

An ace in less than a month, and twice wounded in combat, Flavio Baracchini was faithful to his middle name of Torello ('little bull'). Born in Villafranca Lunigiana on 28 July 1895, he joined the Army in 1914 after technical school and was soon transferred to flying school.

Like other future aces, Barrachini gained experience flying with reconnaissance units, and as an aspirante in

Sottotenente Baracchini (far right) and senior officers pose with Nieuport 11 2179 at Borgnano airfield in the spring of 1917. This may have been the aircraft that Baracchini was flying when he had his first unsuccessful combat on 24 April – he brought the fighter home riddled with bullet holes. Baracchini subsequently commented, 'I still have something to learn'. He was clearly a good student, for less than a month later, on 20 May, he shot down his first victim (*Aeronautica Militare Italiana*)

1916, he flew over the Isonzo Front in a Voisin pusher of *7ª Squadriglia* (renamed *26ª Squadriglia* from 15 April). Although a tough machine, the Voisin was a virtual sitting duck in aerial combat. Yet Baracchini did not hesitate to attack enemy fighters on 14 July and 6 August, and his opportunities to achieve success in combat increased when he joined *81ª Squadriglia* at the front in April 1917 after completing fighter training.

It was while flying the Nieuport 11 that he gained his first victory on 20 May, which he shared with Pier Ruggiero Piccio. Their victim, a Br C I, crashed in flames near Mount Vodice. Shy and quiet on the ground, Baracchini became a fury in the air, downing his fifth victim on 6 June and his tenth on 29 July. By that time he had transferred to *76ª Squadriglia* and was flying the SPAD VII. His rich vein of aerial success was ended on 8 August by a bullet fired from the observer of the 12th aircraft he downed (an unknown two-seater), which broke his jaw. As the blood from the wound soaked his scarf, Baracchini was able to reach the Italian lines and land, after which he was confined to hospital in Udine. Whilst here he received the *Medaglia d'Oro al Valor Militare*.

Baracchini was later sent home on leave to spend months recovering his strength and making daily visits to the dentist. One day, whilst travelling on a train wearing his stylish black uniform and polished boots, and wrapped up to the nose in his cloak, two officers in grey-green field uniforms began making loud comments about shirkers and their 'dandy' dress. Baracchini simply stood up and unlaced his cloak to display both the ugly scar on his chin and the blue ribbon of the Gold Medal. The officers apologised profusely and embraced him.

This Nieuport 17bis (one of the few used by the Italians) displays the 'black shield of d'Artagnan', as Baracchini called his insignia. The aircraft was equipped with a nose-mounted synchronised Vickers machine gun and a Lewis gun mounted on the upper wing. The French cockades on the wings were removed once the aircraft was in Italy, and these are barely visible in this photograph

Baracchini was unable to return to his unit, now based in Casoni, until March 1918. The wound had done nothing to extinguish his aggression, however. Indeed, the long break had sharpened his will to fight, and possibly also to become the top-scoring Italian fighter pilot, as the four aces insignia painted on his Hanriot HD 1 515 seemed to suggest. Back in action, Baracchini had taken his score to 16 victories by 31 May, at which point he returned to *81ª Squadriglia*.

Baracchini poses in front of one of the few SPAD VIIs to be used by *76ª Squadriglia* at Borgnano in the early summer of 1917, just weeks before his face was permanently disfigured by a bullet wound to the jaw. Baracchini probably scored victories on 17 and 29 July and 3 and 8 August while flying this aircraft. The colour of the squadron number painted aft of the roundel remains unknown, but it was possibly yellow or blue (*Roberto Gentilli*)

In June, during the final Austrian offensive of the war, Baracchini used Le Prieur rockets to attack *Drachen* balloons, claiming one on 21 June near San Pietro. But luck deserted him once again four days later after a victorious combat in the company of Sergente Corti. As he crossed the frontline heading back to base, Baracchini was struck in the belly by a bullet fired from the ground. Although barely able to return to his airfield, Baracchini's physical strength helped him recover from a wound which, in an era before antibiotics, was rarely survivable.

On leaving the Army, Baracchini initially attempted to sell surplus military aircraft to Turkey, which was then at war with Greece, before eventually founding a company that manufactured signal rockets for the armed forces. On 29 July 1928, Baracchini was in his factory testing a new explosive when it detonated. Badly burned, the ace was rushed to hospital and then to the clinic of Professor Bastianelli, a leading specialist and also a pilot. Baracchini had survived two years of war and two serious wounds, but now every treatment tried on him proved to be ineffective. After 20 days of agony, the ace died on 18 August.

Flavio Baracchini's main awards – one Gold and one Silver Medal for Military Valour

It should be noted that the 1919 official schedule of confirmed victories awarded Baracchini 20 kills, while the letter sent to the ace by the intelligence branch of the Comando Generale di Aeronautica *credited him with 21. It is possible that the claim of 22 June 1918 was confirmed only after the first list had been compiled.*

Flavio Baracchini's victories

Victory	Date	Location	Victim	Notes
1	20/5/17	Aisovizza	Br C I 129.46 – *Flik* 23	With Piccio
2	23/5/17	unknown	Unknown aircraft	
3	25/5/17	Aisovizza	Unknown aircraft	
4	3/6/17	Sober	Br C I 129.02 – *Flik* 4	
5	6/6/17	Vodice	Br C I 229.19 – *FIG* 1, Kpl Alexander Vezsprémy and Ltn Ernst Pirnos both KIA	
6	18/6/17	Aisovizza	Br C I 129.14 – *Flik* 32	
7	19/6/17	Aisovizza	Br C I 29.63 – *Flik* 19	
8	22/6/17	San Marco	Br C I 229.05 – *Flik* 35	
9	17/7/17	Lom	Br C I 129.57 – *Flik* 12	
10	29/7/17	Tomino	Br C I unknown – *Flik* 2	
11	3/8/17	Val di Sava	Unknown aircraft	With Baracca
12	8/8/17	Tolmino	Unknown two-seater	
13	3/5/18	Sernaglia	Unknown fighter	
14	13/5/18	Arcade	Albatros D III 153.189 – *Flik* 68/J	
15	20/5/18	Sernaglia	Albatros D III 153.163 – *Flik* 42/J	
16	26/5/18	Cimadolmo	Albatros D III unknown – *Flik* 42/J	
17	15/6/18	Moriago	Br C I 369.113 – *Flik* 38/D	
18	15/6/18	Montello	Unknown aircraft	With Mazzucco
19	21/6/18	San Pietro	*Drachen* – BK 4	
20	22/6/18	Montello	Albatros D III unknown – *Flik* 42/J	
21	25/6/18	Motta di Livenza	Unknown fighter	With Corti

Sebastiano Bedendo

Sebastiano Bedendo was born in
Rovigo, near the mouth of the River
Po, on 18 July 1895. Drafted when
Italy entered the war, he served
briefly with an artillery regiment
and was later assigned to a kite balloon unit as an observer. Earning his
wings in the summer of 1916,
Tenente Bedendo was assigned to
fly reconnaissance missions on the
Northern and Isonzo Fronts, and
did not reach a fighter unit until
after the Caporetto retreat.

As a fighter pilot, Bedendo
returned to action over the Northern Front in November 1917, often
transferring between *71ª* and *72ª*
Squadriglia. He did not achieve his
first victory until 29 July 1918,

Sebastiano Bedendo (right) and his
pilot are seen here in the front seat
of a Maurice Farman 14 pusher. This
photograph was probably taken in
the summer of 1917 during flight
training at Busto Arsizio, near
Varese. Bedendo is armed with a
Mauser pistol fitted with a wooden
butt and a box to collect spent cases
to avoid damage to the aft-mounted
propeller (*Rozzi*)

when he downed an unidentified fighter attempting to attack the Pomilio
PE reconnaissance aircraft that he was escorting. The following day
Bedendo destroyed an unidentified aircraft over Monte Cadria, and on
the 31st, during yet another Pomilio escort, he shared in the destruction
of a third aircraft with Capitano Breglia. On 6 August Bedendo was
patrolling over Tonezza when he attacked a fighter that he duly sent down
trailing a long yellow plume of smoke. He subsequently 'made ace' on 22
August when he shared his final victory with Breglia over Noviglio. On
20 October Bedendo joined the prestigious *Squadriglia Baracca*, as *91ª*
had been named following the death of the 'ace of aces', and he
participated in the unit's last offensive of the war.

Returning to civilian life, Bedendo completed his engineering studies
at university and upon graduating joined the engineering branch of the
newly-formed *Regia Aeronautica* in 1924. In 1933 he used the Nuvoli
N.5 light aircraft to set two world records for machines of this class. After
one of the records was beaten by a French Farman 239, Bedendo
recaptured it in 1935 flying the improved Nuvoli N.5RR. Tragically, on
24 August 1935 Giovanni Testore, Giovanni Nicastro and Sebastiano
Bedendo were killed when Nuvoli N.5 Cab I-NUBE lost a wing and
crashed near Spinosa di Ottiglio.

Sebastiano Bedendo's main awards – one Silver Medal for Military
Valour

Sebastiano Bedendo's victories

Victory	Date	Location	Victim	Notes
1	29/7/18	Val Terragnolo	Unknown fighter	
2	30/7/18	Monte Cadria	Unknown aircraft	
3	31/7/18	Calliano	Unknown aircraft	With Breglia
4	6/8/18	Tonezza	Unknown fighter	With Vecco
5	22/8/18	Noviglio	Unknown aircraft	With Breglia

Aldo Bocchese

Aldo Bocchese was born in Milan on 23 December 1894. At the time he was drafted into military service he was working as clerk, and this meant that he spent the first two years of the war as an accountant. In March 1917 Bocchese volunteered for flying duties, and following training he was sent to *70ª Squadriglia* on 20 January 1918 with the rank of sergente.

On 17 April he, Avet and Eleuteri scored their first victories together, claiming two fighters and a two-seater. The trio then claimed a double victory on the morning of 15 July. During this combat Bocchese fired on an enemy fighter, which spun away, but he was then forced to defend himself from another aircraft that had latched onto his tail. Bocchese quickly turned defence into attack, getting in behind his assailant and firing several bursts at the enemy machine. He followed the latter down to an altitude of 400 m (1300 ft) before breaking off his pursuit.

Boasting excellent eyesight, Bocchese was often asked to lead patrols, despite being a non-commissioned officer. His sixth, and last, victory came on 28 October during the Vittorio Veneto battle when he, Avet and and Eleuteri engaged an Aviatik D I of *Flik* 70/K. Despite suffering from jammed machine guns, Bocchese helped his squadronmates force the two-seater to land in Italian territory near Arcade.

After being discharged in 1919, Bocchese was recalled to service post-war, but in a non-flying capacity. In May 1940, just a month before Italy entered World War 2, he was finally discharged due to failing health. Remaining in touch with his old wartime comrades, Bocchese lived quietly firstly in Rome and then in Lastra a Signa, near Florence, where he died on 15 March 1976. In accordance with his last will, he was buried wearing his military decorations.

Sergente Aldo Bocchese laughs as he dons his leather jacket prior to heading off on a patrol in the last months of the war. Behind him is Hanriot HD 1 19209, which was built by Macchi and sent to the front in July 1918. The fighter was later operated by *70ª Squadriglia* from Gazzo airfield, before being retired to the aircraft depot at Poggio Renatico (*Roberto Gentilli*)

Aldo Bocchese's main awards – one Bronze Medal for Military Valour

Aldo Bocchese's victories

Victory	Date	Location	Victim	Notes
1	17/4/18	Valdobbiadene	Br C I 169.35 – *Flik* 52/D	With Avet and Eleuteri
2	17/4/18	Valdobbiadene	Albatros D III 153.152 – *Flik* 42/J	With Avet and Eleuteri
3	17/4/18	Valdobbiadene	Albatros D III unknown – *Flik* 42/J	With Avet and Eleuteri
4	15/7/18	Vidor	Aviatik D I 38.63 – *Flik* 74/J	
5	15/7/18	Sernaglia	Unknown fighter	With Avet and Eleuteri
6	28/10/18	Arcade	Aviatik D I – *Flik* 70/K	With Avet and Eleuteri

Alessandro Buzio

Alessandro Buzio was born in Pavia on 13 January 1893. During his youth he studied as an accountant, but he was also a strong swimmer and rode motorcycles. For a young man keen on sports and machines, volunteering for aviation after the draft was an obvious choice. Having gained his military flying licence, and following brief service as an instructor, Buzio was assigned to the newly-formed *75ª Squadriglia* in Verona.

He arrived at the front in April 1916, and on 27 June scored his first victory over an Austrian Br C I. That day, Sottotenente Buzio, Tenente De Bernardi (later an outstanding test pilot and winner of the 1926

Schneider Trophy) and Sergente Nardini were all on standby at Consonni when a cannon shot alerted them to the fact a Br C I was approaching Verona. They quickly intercepted the enemy aircraft and forced it down near Arzignano. The victors were not only awarded a medal but also a cash prize that had been offered by local businessmen. This was promptly donated to a veterans' support fund.

After an uneventful year, Buzio was transferred nearer to the front with a posting to *81ª Squadriglia* at Borgnano. On 31 July 1917, whilst patrolling over Mount Sabotino, he attacked a two-seater which tried to dive away after Buzio's first bursts. He gave chase, but his Hanriot HD 1 was overtaken by a faster SPAD VII flown by Baracca – the latter administered the *coup de grace*, thus giving him his 15th victory.

Following the Italian retreat, Buzio left *81ª Squadriglia* for *76ª Squadriglia*. He claimed his first victory with the unit while flying his Hanriot on 19 December, and one week later participated in the Istrana air battle, but claimed no successes. His first victory of 1918 came on 3 May when Buzio, leading four squadronmates, claimed a Br C I over the Brenta canal. On the evening of 21 June it was the turn of Aviatik D I 115.31 of *Flik* 68/J to be shot down near Mandre 'after repeated bursts of machine gun fire'. Buzio shared his fifth victory with Silvio Scaroni. He escaped unhurt when, on 15 July, his Hanriot was rammed by a British RE 8 while taxying at Casoni airfield. In September Buzio left the front to serve as an instructor. He saw no further action in World War 1.

Between the wars Buzio worked for the airline *Aviolinee Italiane*, while also rising in rank within the air force reserve, although he never returned to flying duties. Buzio died in Milan on 1 October 1972.

Alessandro Buzio's main awards – two Silver and one Bronze Medals for Military Valour

Alessandro Buzio (left) poses with a Nieuport scout at Cascina Costa, where he was trained to fly fighters in the spring of 1916. Standing alongside him is future ace Luigi Olivi, who had been sent to the training unit from a reconnaissance squadron, and who would ultimately be assigned to *76ª Squadriglia*. Buzio would also serve with this unit, but by the time he was transferred in during the autumn of 1917 Olivi had been killed in a flying accident. To the right is Capitano Mario Gordesco, who would later command the Aerial Gunnery School at Furbara, near Rome, and subsequently perish at the controls of an SVA at Bakshir, in the Ural Mountains, whilst trying to fly from Rome to Tokyo in 1920

Alessandro Buzio's victories

Victory	Date	Location	Victim	Notes
1	27/6/16	Arzignano	Br C I 26.11 – *Flik* 21, Zgsf Josef Holub and Fahn edler von Langer both wounded in action	With De Bernardi, Nardini & Consonni
2	31/7/17	Podgora	Br C I 69.93 – *Flik* 46	
3	19/12/17	Val Seren	Unknown aircraft	With Avenati & Donati
4	3/5/18	Asolone	Br C I 169.78 – *Flik* 16/D	
5	21/6/18	Mandre	Aviatik D I 115.31 – *Flik* 68/J	

Ernesto Cabruna

Ernesto Cabruna was born on 2 June 1889 in the city of Tortona, in Piedmont, into a family of shopkeepers. He attended technical school, and in 1907 volunteered for the *Reali Carabinieri* (military police, which was also charged with general law enforcement duties). Cabruna distinguished himself in 1908 during relief operations after an earthquake which devastated the Sicilian city of Messina, causing 120,000 deaths. His efforts in the Libyan War and the Italian occupation of the Aegean Islands also brought praise from his superiors.

Wearing a balaclava, Ernesto Cabruna is seen here standing in front of Nieuport 11 2129 of *84ª Squadriglia* at San Maria la Longa airfield in the summer of 1917 (*Fotomuseo Panini*)

When Italy entered World War 1, Cabruna volunteered for service at the front, and he received his first Bronze Medal for his courage while caring for wounded soldiers during an Austrian bombardment of Asiago. His application for pilot training was accepted in May 1916, and Cabruna gained his wings five months later. Like other future aces, he was at first assigned to a reconnaissance unit (*29ª Squadriglia*), where he remained until sent to fighter school in April 1917. Initially posted to *84ª Squadriglia*, Cabruna returned to the Isonzo Front in July with *80ª Squadriglia*.

His first victory came during the dark days of Caporetto when, on 26 October, he and three squadronmates shared in the destruction of an Austrian K212 seaplane near Lake Doberdò, in the Carso region. By 12 March 1918 Cabruna had scored three victories, but it was the combat of 29 March which made him the subject of the cover art of the weekly magazine *Domenica del Corriere* – famous Italian artist Achille Beltrame chose to portray Cabruna's dogfight in one of his celebrated illustrations.

That day, while flying between Ponte di Piave and Grisolera, Cabruna left his formation and bounced a patrol of ten enemy aircraft. While the enemy wingmen scattered, Cabruna got on to the tail of the leader – he described it as 'a red aeroplane' – and fired several bursts. The red machine dived steeply into the fog, but Cabruna did not follow him

Cabruna (left) with friend, and fellow ace, Alvaro Leonardi pose with the former's SPAD VII 1420. The fighter displays both the red heart insignia of *77ª Squadriglia* and the crest of Cabruna's home town of Tortona. This photograph was probably taken at Marcon, where the unit was based from October 1917 through to war's end (*Roberto Gentilli*)

because of the rest of the patrol circling above. In fact, all but three of the Austrian wingmen had followed their leader into the undercast, with the trio of scouts that remained above the fog following them down almost immediately once the rest of the Italian patrol appeared on the scene. Once back at their airfield, Cabruna's squadronmates cheered his bravery in chasing after the red fighter, but he just quietly asked for a cigarette! Although observers on

the ground could only confirm his victim had entered a dive, the claim was verified. Even today, Austrian sources cannot confirm the loss, but Cabruna had clearly demonstrated his lack of fear in single-handedly attacking a superior formation.

Cabruna added two more victories to his tally during the final Austrian offensive, on 15 and 20 June. That summer he was commissioned and promoted to the rank of sottotenente on 28 July in recognition of his success. However, on 26 September Cabruna was involved in a flying accident that almost ended his career. Having completed a sortie in a new Ansaldo A.1 Balilla (the first fighter of Italian design), he was coming in to land at Castenedolo airfield when hot oil squirted into his face and Cabruna lost control and crashed. Despite being taken to hospital suffering from a broken shoulder and minor injuries, he was declared fit for combat – with his shoulder still bandaged up – on 30 October. Cabruna scored his last two victories on 2 November when he downed two of six enemy aircraft taking off from Aiello airfield.

During his career Cabruna had shown that he was no mere 'yes man' and submissive executor of orders. He proved this again in 1919 when he followed the flamboyant poet d'Annunzio to Fiume (now Rijeka, in Croatia) to fight in a rebellion *against* the Italian government. When this adventure ended, Cabruna had no money and no job, in the army or elsewhere. After a period of depression, he rejoined the army and was awarded the *Medaglia d'Oro al Valor Militare* for his war service. Cabruna was eventually discharged due to ill health in 1932 . He gradually became disillusioned with Fascism to the extent that during World War 2 he was listed in British intelligence documents as a supporter of the 'Free Italy' movement under the *nom de guerre* 'X-19'. After the war Cabruna chose to live in isolation, and he died on 9 January 1960.

Ernesto Cabruna's main awards – one Gold and one Silver Medal for Military Valour

This photograph shows to advantage the large Italian cockade and the Roman numeral XIII on the upper wings of SPAD VII 1420. After the war the army donated aircraft to the airmen who had received the *Medaglia d'Oro al Valor Militare,* and as a result several machines survived to be put on display in Italian aviation museums. This SPAD VII is one such aircraft, the fighter having been donated to Cabruna in the livery seen here. This priceless machine was displayed for many years in Tortona, but in the late 1960s it was moved to the Italian Air Force Museum in Vigna di Valle, near Rome

Ernesto Cabruna's victories

Victory	Date	Location	Victim	Notes
1	26/10/17	Doberdò Lake	K212 seaplane, Frg Ltn M Kramer von Drauberg died of wounds and Flgmr Marcello Anasipoli PoW	With Ancillotto, Leonardi & Lombardi
2	5/12/17	Salgareda	Br C I 69.17 – *Flik* 32/B	
3	12/3/18	San Donà	Aviatik C I 214.04 – *Flik* 49/D	
4	29/3/18	Ponte di Piave	Unknown 'red' fighter	
5	15/6/18	Tezze	Albatros D III 153.211 – *Flik* 51/J	
6	20/6/18	San Donà	Br C I 329.39 – *Flik* 22/D, pilot unknown	
7	2/11/18	Aiello	Unknown aircraft	
8	2/11/18	Aiello	Unknown aircraft	

Umberto Calvello

The son of a general and grandson of an admiral of the Kingdom of the Two Sicilies, Umberto Calvello was born in Pistoia, Tuscany, on 28 May 1897. In 1916 he enlisted in the *Regia Marina* and was soon posted to the Venice Seaplane Station as an observer. Assigned to *251ª Squadriglia*, Calvello earned a *Medaglia di Bronzo* for 'daring and exemplary prowess' displayed while returning to his base after an attack on Trieste during the stormy night of 30 June 1917. Promoted to guardiamarina, he learned to fly during the summer of 1917 and, after the Italian retreat to the River Piave, flew five operational missions in October and 13 in November.

During this period the Italian Navy was forming its first fighter units, which it equipped with Macchi M.5s. Calvello was transferred to *260ª Squadriglia*, although he remained in Venice. The following months were uneventful, allowing the young officer to refine his skills in relative safety. On 22 April Calvello and two colleagues escorted a seaplane that had been sent to attack the Austrian battleship *Tegetthof*, which was conducting gunnery practice off Fasana. During the course of the mission the escorts attacked the Austrian seaplane R1, which was conducting an anti-submarine patrol. It was shot down after a lengthy combat.

The M.5 represented a formidable adversary for the Austrian seaplanes, and on 4 May the fighters from Venice scored a great victory against their opponents from Trieste, who were led by the Imperial ace Gottfried von Banfield. The Italian patrol, under the leadership of Tenente di Vascello Martinengo, was escorting a camera-equipped M.5 towards Trieste when it encountered several seaplanes identified as 'Abwehr' types. In the ensuing dogfight Calvello and his comrades downed A91 and A78 near some Italian torpedo boats, while Banfield was forced to put his A82 down near the shore.

In the summer months Calvello flew several night missions to deliver homing pigeons to Italian agents operating behind enemy lines. His squadronmate in these dangerous missions was another daring and skilled pilot, Sottotenente di Vascello Ivo Ravazzoni.

During the Vittorio Veneto battle even the flying boats attacked the retreating enemy. On 31 October 1918, Calvello was strafing enemy troops near Caorle when his Macchi was hit and he was forced to land in a swamp. While other M.5s kept the soldiers at bay, Ravazzoni came down to rescue his friend. They pierced the hull of the damaged fighter in order to sink it, then Calvello took control of the other Macchi, with Ravazzoni perched on the fuselage holding onto the engine struts. After a long take-off run the makeshift two-seater staggered into the air and skimmed the reeds, pursued by Austrian rifle bullets.

The boy-faced ace who once stole fruit from orchards in Venice and handled the M.5 with such a light

Guardiamarina Calvello poses with two of his mechanics on the apron of *Stazione Idrovolanti 'Giuseppe Miraglia'*, in Venice. Calvello chose the popular 'Happy Hooligan' (called *Fortunello*, or Lucky Man, by the Italians) for display on his fighter's nose, but here the normally gentle character drawn by Frederick Burr Opper marches aggressively toward the enemy screaming in the Venetian dialect *'Ocio! Ocio! Fiol d'un can!'* ('Look out! Look out! Son of a bitch!'). The futurist motto *'Marciare non marcire'* (March! Don't rot!) can just be made out on *Fortunello's* suitcase (*Roberto Gentilli*)

Calvello is seen here sat on the hull of A91 – a W 18 flying boat built by Hansa Brandenburg – which he helped bring down on 4 May 1918. The plywood fuselage shows damage from the Vickers bullets fired by the Italian M.5s. The aircraft was forced to ditch in the sea, after which it was towed to Venice along with its pilot, Ltn Josef Niedermayer. The latter had also been shot down just three days earlier by Orazio Pierozzi and other Italian naval pilots of *261ª Squadriglia*. The narrow channel which separated San Andrea Island from the mainland is visible in the background to the right. This stretch of waterway was used by Italian seaplanes when both taking off and alighting

touch died on 10 August 1919 when the SIAI S.9 flying-boat that he was flying crashed following engine trouble.

Calvello's flight log records only three victories, although his name was included in the official list of aces released by the *Regia Marina*. The reasons for this remain unknown, although the missing victories may have been overlooked because of the loss of relevant records. Quite apart from his final tally, Calvello still deserves a place in this book, and in the almost forgotten history of the Italian naval air service in World War 1.

Umberto Calvello's main awards – two Silver Medals for Military Valour

Umberto Calvello's victories

Victory	Date	Place	Victim	Notes
1	22/4/18	Fasana	R1 Seaplane, Sfr Alfred edler von Herbetz and NH Stefan Bauer both captured unhurt	With Rivieri & Pagliacci
2	4/5/18	Trieste	A91 seaplane, Ltn Josef Niedermayer PoW	With Jannello, Martinengo, Pagliacci & Rivieri
3	4/5/18	Trieste	A78 seaplane	
4	4/5/18	Trieste	A82 seaplane	

Marziale Cerutti

The lively and easygoing boy, the daring motorcycle rider and the joker whose pranks scandalised the peaceful people of Lonato, in Lombardia, where he lived with his family was born in Brescia on 10 March 1895. In 1915 Marziale Cerutti volunteered for the army, but he enlisted as a humble private soldier to avoid the time-consuming paperwork involved in applying to be an officer. After brief service as a driver, he was accepted for flying training.

In November 1916 he was assigned as a caporale to *79ª Squadriglia*, which flew Nieuport 11s on patrols over the mountainous terrain of the Asiago plateau region. After some skirmishes Cerutti, who, like the French ace Nungesser wore a stocking under his leather flying helmet, scored his first victory on 14 June 1917. He wrote in his combat report;

'At about 0800hr, cruising between Cima Caldiera and Asiago, I saw an enemy aeroplane of the Albatros type flying at my altitude of 3800 m

Marziale Cerutti smiles as he poses with a Nieuport 11, which displays the Italian national colours on its engine cowling. In a letter, Baracca called him 'gallant' and 'very promising', but also used the term 'lost soul' to describe the personality of his comrade. Endowed with a bizarre sense of humour, Cerutti invited some friends to drive with him to Lake Garda for a swim before the war and then promptly drove his automobile into the water at full speed! Such was his notoriety that a wealthy and religious aunt explicitly disinherited him in her will (*Roberto Gentilli*)

One of the last Nieuport 27s used by Cerutti during the war displayed the letters 'MIR' on its fuselage sides. These stood for *'Marziale Imperatore Romano'* (Roman Emperor Marziale). The fighter was also adorned with the ace of clubs insignia. The Nieuport 27 was not particularly liked by Italian pilots due to its poor build quality. Indeed, many of the newly-delivered aircraft supplied from France needed a complete overhaul before they could be accepted for service. Complaints ranged from twisted airframes to screws that he been hammered home (*Fotomuseo Panini*)

(12,350 ft) near Mount Verena. The enemy came resolutely towards me and opened fire at a distance of about 300 m (325 yrd). Manoeuvring to attack, my aircraft sideslipped for about 50 m (55 yrd) and I was able to get onto the tail of my opponent and open fire. The enemy aircraft turned to reach friendly territory and I followed, firing further bursts. After about 50 rounds, I saw the aircraft bank over on its right wing in a swift descent. I continued to follow, unloading the rest of my twin magazines, until we reached an altitude of 3000 m. The enemy continued its fall to the ground. It must have crashed near Vezzena.'

Two days later, Cerutti was promoted to sergente. On 24 November he scored a double victory which earned him not only a Silver Medal 'in the field', but also praise from Baracca. Cerutti was bounced by a bold enemy pilot probably flying a German two-seater on 27 November, but he was able to reverse the position and hit his opponent's fuel tank. This success made him an ace. His tenth victory came on 21 June 1918, and on 4 July Cerutti claimed a *Drachen* between Oderzo and Fontanelle. He achieved his last victory, over a fighter, on 27 October near Cittadella di Piave.

As with many other airmen, Cerutti's long war service had taken its toll on his health to the point where the ace was admitted to hospital in January 1919 suffering from nervous exhaustion. He remained in the military and was promoted to sottotenente that same year. By the time Italy entered World War 2 Cerutti had a family – he had married a German woman and they had two sons – and attained the rank of general.

After the Italian armistice, he briefly joined the *Aeronautica Nazionale Repubblicana* – the air force of the *Repubblica Sociale Italiana*, which was the puppet state in the areas of northern Italy that were still occupied by the Germans. Cerutti was quickly dismissed, however, so he decided to collaborate in secret with the Italian Resistance in the area. When the war ended he lost his rank due to his previous allegiance with the Fascist Republic, and he was killed in a motorcycle accident before he could clear his name. Cerutti had assembled a machine from parts, and on 26 May 1946, while attempting to avoid a woman in the street near his home, he crashed and was killed. Cerutti was posthumously acquitted of all charges and his rank reinstated.

Marziale Cerutti's main awards – three Silver Medals for Military Valour

Marziale Cerutti's victories

Victory	Date	Place	Victim	Notes
1	14/6/17	Monte Verena	KD 28.35 – *Flik* 21	
2	26/10/17	Volzana	Unknown aircraft	With Poli
3	24/11/17	Fonzaso	Br C I 29.05 – *Flik* 24/F	
4	24/11/17	Monte Grappa	Br C I 229.16 – *Flik* 17/D	
5	27/11/17	Alano	Unknown two-seater	
6	28/1/18	Asiago	Unknown fighter	
7	28/1/18	Val Ronchi	Unknown fighter	With Reali
8	11/2/18	Asiago	Phönix D I 328.06 – *Flik* 24	
9	24/2/18	Crespano	Phönix D I 128.09 – *Flik* 39/D	
10	21/6/18	Susegana	Br C I 269.22 – *Flik* 65/DS	
11	21/6/18	Susegana	Unknown two-seater	With Reali & Toffoletti
12	21/6/18	Susegana	Unknown two-seater	With Reali & Toffoletti
13	24/6/18	Ponte alla Priula	Br C I 369.67 – *Flik* 4/D	
14	4/7/18	Oderzo	*Drachen* – unit unknown	
15	11/9/18	Ponte alla Priula	Unknown aircraft	
16	26/10/18	Mandre	Aviatik D I 338.26 – *Flik* 74/J	
17	27/10/18	Cittadella di Piave	Unknown fighter – *Flik* 74/J	With Rennella

Antonio Chiri

Born on 26 August 1894, Antonio Chiri was the son of a miller. He emigrated to France as a teenager, but returned to Italy upon the outbreak of World War 1 to be conscripted into an artillery regiment. Chiri soon volunteered for the air service and received his wings in May 1916. After serving with other units, he was assigned in November to *78ª Squadriglia* as a sergente pilota.

Chiri scored his first victory on 19 March 1917 when he opened fire at point-blank range on Br C I 27.55 flying over the Asiago plateau. The enemy aircraft was forced to land. Another victory came on 26 August, but it was not until late in the year that Chiri added three more aircraft to his tally – a two-seater on 13 November and two more reconnaissance types in December, including one during the Istrana air battle. Although Chiri continued to fly until war's end, he scored only one more confirmed victory (on 31 August 1918).

Antonio Chiri poses alongside his first victim, Br C I 27.55 of *Flik* 21. On 19 March 1917 this Phönix-built aircraft was attacked by Chiri while he was flying Nieuport 11 1664 on a patrol over Asiago Plateau. Hit several times in the fuel tank, radiator and engine, the two-seater was able to crash-land near Rotzo and was captured, along with its crew. This event was reported in the following day's *Bollettino di Guerra*, and earned Chiri the first of his three *Medaglia d'Argento al Valor Militare*

Chiri chose to distinguish himself in the air by flying black-tailed Hanriots from December 1917 onward. This French-built aircraft was the last Hanriot assigned to the ace, and he was at the controls when it crashed while taking off from San Giacomo di Veglia airfield on 21 December 1918. The cause of the accident was almost certainly incorrectly rigged flying controls. The fighter crashed from low altitude, killing some bystanders who had gathered to watch the take-off and leaving Chiri in a coma (*Roberto Gentilli*)

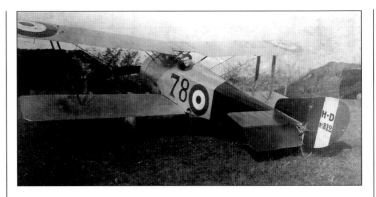

Inexplicably, Chiri is credited with five victories in the official list, although other documents credit him with six.

On 21 December 1918 he took off from San Giacomo di Veglia airfield, but his Hanriot HD 1 812 suffered a control malfunction and crashed, killing some bystanders and putting the pilot in hospital. Chiri was in a coma until 6 January 1919. Discharged from the Army in 1920, he transferred to the air force reserve and began working for the Italian postal service in Turin – by the time he retired he was provincial director. He died on 6 January 1971.

Antonio Chiri's main awards – three Silver Medals for Military Valour

Antonio Chiri's victories

Victory	Date	Location	Victim	Notes
1	19/3/17	Gallio	Br C I 27.55 – *Flik* 21	
2	26/8/17	Lokve	Unknown fighter	
3	13/11/17	Arcade	Unknown two-seater – *FA (A)* 232	
4	10/12/17	Noventa	Aviatik C I 37.24 – *Flik* 58	
5	26/12/17	Montebelluna	German DFW C V – unit unknown	Shared with several Italian and Allied airmen
6	31/8/18	Mandre	Ufag C I 161.107 – *Flik* 22/D	With Fucini & Rennella

Bartolomeo Costantini

Of slender build, with his hair slicked back and a perennial cigarette held between his fingers, Bartolomeo Costantini cut a dashing figure as a man who had a true passion for speed. Born in Vittorio Veneto on 14 February 1889, the young 'Meo' fell in love with aviation and volunteered for the Army, obtaining his pilot's licence on 13 September 1912.

Initially, Tenente Costantini flew the already-venerable Bleriot, before converting onto the new Nieuport 11 fighter. On 12 August 1916 he was assigned to *78ª Squadriglia*, but the Asiago Front was quiet at this time and he had to wait until spring 1917, when he was assigned to the new *91ª Squadriglia* formed by Baracca, to see some real action. Costantini flew many escort and photographic reconnaissance missions, but his first victory did not come until the days of Caporetto.

On 25 October, Costantini, now a capitano, and Ruffo shared in the destruction of a German two-seater near Tolmino. The enemy aircraft was identified as an 'Aviatik', which was the name given by Italians to the

Wearing a leather flying suit, 'Meo' Costantini (left) enjoys a cigarette in front of a *78ª Squadriglia* Nieuport 17. He appears to be totally unconcerned about the risk of igniting petrol fumes escaping from the scout's fuel tank as it is filled immediately behind him! Just as oblivious to this potential hazard are Sottotenente Giovanni Brenta (centre) and the various mechanics tending the fighter (*Bernardo Sclerandi*)

78ª Squadriglia had used flags as its insignia, and Costantini recalled his old unit by choosing a black pennant as his personal marking when he moved to *91ª Squadriglia*. He scored four of his six confirmed victories while flying the SPAD VII. Costantini also served as squadron CO in December 1917 when Baracca was sent to tour aircraft factories that month, accompanied by Ruffo and Piccio (*Roberto Gentilli*)

German DFW C V, and it was followed by another (shared with Fanti) the following day near Castelmonte. Costantini claimed two more victories over German aircraft on 23 and 30 November, but then all aerial activity slowed. Indeed, he would have to wait until 12 August 1918 to score his all-important fifth victory – a Phönix D I. Ten days later, Costantini downed his final victim near Marano di Piave. The Italian saw

During the final months of the war Costantini flew the more powerful and better-armed SPAD XIII. This photograph was probably taken at Quinto di Treviso airfield, where *91ª Squadriglia* deployed on 11 March 1918 from Padua. An Austrian air raid on the night of 20/21 February put no fewer than 13 SPADs out of service. *91ª* remained at Quinto until the end of the war, when it moved to the former Austro-Hungarian airfield at Zaule, near Trieste (*Roberto Gentilli*)

the enemy airman jump from the cockpit of his Albatros D III as the aircraft fell away in flames and then spotted a parachute open. *91ª Squadriglia's* war diary reported the event with the comment, 'It was the first time that a parachute had been put to practical use in an aircraft'.

When the war ended Costantini had logged 180 operational missions. Returning to his beloved racing cars, after competing in several events at the wheel of a Bugatti, he was invited to the Mulhouse factory in 1921 by Ettore Bugatti himself and offered the job of test driver and sporting director. Costantini subsequently enjoyed numerous successes, and twice competed in Sicily's *Targa Florio*, but the death of a fellow driver induced him to retire. Costantini continued to work in the Bugatti engineering department until 1937, when he moved to Alfa Romeo. There, he was appointed technical commercial inspector and later head of preparation in the racing division. In the meantime, he had reached the rank of tenente colonnello in the air force reserve. Costantini contracted a serious illness in 1941 and died in Milan on 19 July. He was just 52 years old.

Bartolomeo Costantini's main awards – two Silver Medals for Military Valour

Bartolomeo Costantini's victories

Victory	Date	Location	Victim	Notes
1	25/10/17	Tolmino	German DFW – several possibilities	With Ruffo
2	26/10/17	Castelmonte	German DFW – several possibilities	With Fanti
3	23/11/17	Cornuda	Unknown aircraft	
4	30/11/17	Rivasecca	German DFW – *Fl Abt* 14	With Bacula & Olivero
5	12/8/18	S. Lucia di Piave	Phönix D I 128.11 – *Flik* 40/P	
6	22/8/18	Mareno	Albatros D III 253.71 – *Flik* 42/J	

Leopoldo Eleuteri

Leopoldo Eleuteri was born in Castel Ritaldi, in Central Italy, on 17 December 1894 and later attended technical school. After the Italian declaration of war he was conscripted, but served initially as a clerk. Eleuteri volunteered for flying duties, and on 26 March 1917 he was awarded his pilot's wings. Assigned to a reconnaissance squadron, Sottotenente Eleuteri flew many missions, and he even survived a close encounter with the famed *Flik* 55 *Kaiserstaffel* on 18 November 1917. He and his observer, Tenente Velo, were flying over the Asiago Plateau when their SAML was attacked by Austrian aces Arigi, Mayer and Kiss. Their bullets hit the Italian two-seater, one striking the left boot of the observer, but Eleuteri was able to put his aircraft into a violent spin and escape.

Soon afterwards Eleuteri was selected for fighter training, returning to the front in February 1918 with *70ª Squadriglia*. There, he became friendly with aces Avet and Bocchese, and it was while on patrol with them that he scored his first four victories. He then scored with Reali and Lucentini on 4 October, alone on the 8th and again with Avet and Bocchese on the 28th (this would prove to be his final claim). Eleuteri's victory on 8 October came whilst he was flying a new Ansaldo A.1 Balilla (Hunter), and this success is believed to have been the only one credited to Italy's first fighter type to attain series production.

Leopoldo Eleuteri (seated second from right, with pipe and flower) poses with colleagues of *70ª* and *82ª Squadriglia* at Gazzo Padovano immediately after the end of the war. Maggiore Ercole, commander of the *X Gruppo*, is standing in the centre with a scarf around his neck. To his right is Flaminio Avet (in the black leather coat) and immediately behind the latter, half-hidden, is Alessandro Resch. Maggiore Ercole had received a *Medaglia d'Oro al Valor Militare* in 1916 whilst serving as a bomber pilot, having made it back to Italian lines after a march of 50 km (31 miles) following the destruction of his aircraft. He was the only survivor of the bomber's three-man crew *(Avet Family)*

When peace came Eleuteri left the air service for university, and he obtained his engineering degree in 1922. A year later he was admitted to the engineering branch of the *Regia Aeronautica*, and he was also able to resume flying. On 19 January 1926, while flying an Ansaldo AC.2, Eleuteri engaged in a mock dogfight with a Hanriot but the aircraft collided and both pilots were killed.

Leopoldo Eleuteri's main awards – two Silver Medals for Military Valour

Leopoldo Eleuteri's victories

Victory	Date	Location	Victim	Notes
1	17/4/18	Valdobbiadene	Br C I 169.35 – *Flik* 52/D	With Avet & Bocchese
2	17/4/18	Valdobbiadene	Albatros D III 153.152 – *Flik* 42/J	With Avet & Bocchese
3	15/7/18	Vidor	Aviatik D I 38.63 – *Flik* 74/J	With Avet & Bocchese
4	15/7/18	Sernaglia	Unknown fighter	With Avet & Bocchese
5	4/10/18	Moriago	Unknown fighter	With Reali & Lucentini
6	8/10/18	Oderzo	Unknown fighter	
7	28/10/18	Arcade	Unknown Aviatik D I – *Flik* 70/J, pilot unknown	With Avet & Bocchese

Guglielmo Fornagiari

Guglielmo Fornagiari was born on 11 March 1892 in Lizzano, in the Apennines, between Bologna and Florence. He emigrated to France, where he worked as mechanic, before returning to Italy upon being drafted in 1912. Assigned to the air service, Fornagiari was working on Caproni bombers by 1915. He managed to get himself transferred to flying training, and returned to the front in March 1916 as a sergente pilota. Serving initially with *77ª Squadriglia*, Fornagiari subsequently moved to *78ª Squadriglia* and scored his first victory on 22 August 1917.

In the absence of an official victory list, the reconstruction of Fornagiari's score is particularly difficult, but in all probability he had accumulated four confirmed aerial successes by the end of 1917. His fifth

A group of *78ª Squadriglia* pilots scan the sky over Istrana airfield. They are, from left to right, Nicelli, Imolesi, Brenta, unknown, unknown, Fornagiari and unknown. The aircraft in the background is probably Nieuport 11 1664, which was flown by Chiri when he scored his first victory. Its displays the combination of triangles and balls initially used by the unit to identify its aircraft. Fornagiari was taking off from Fossalunga airfield on 27 June 1917 in this aircraft when he saw a woman and a child on the field. To avoid them, he pulled the aircraft up sharply, stalled and crashed into a vineyard, tragically killing two boys

A pennant outlined in white embellishes the fuselage of this Hanriot HD 1, which was probably flown by Fornagiari during the summer of 1918. *78ª Squadriglia* initially adopted a red pennant, but photographs taken in the later stages of the war show several variations on this theme. Some aircraft displayed the flags of Allied nations and, in some cases, there were as many as four flags on the same machine. The colour of the pennant on this example, which bears both the original French number 60 and the Italian serial 6092, is uncertain, being possibly black or blue. The Hanriot was damaged in an air raid on Fossalunga on the night of 1 February 1918 (*Fotomuseo Panini*)

was scored on 27 January 1918 during the combat in which Kpl Gottlieb Munczar and the great ace Josef Kiss (who was also severely wounded) were forced to land. After his sixth and seventh victories on 18 and 21 February, 'Fo-Fo' Fornagiari (as had been nicknamed because of a stutter) flew his 200th mission on 22 February. During the following months Fornagiari continued to fly untiringly, and although he became involved in aerial combats, no further claims were confirmed in the post-war review. That September he was transferred to a second-line unit for a rest, returning to *78ª Squadriglia* in December when the war was over.

Fornagiari stayed in the air force post-war, and from 1923 wore the new blue uniform of the *Regia Aeronautica*. By remaining in his old unit until 1935, Fornagiari set a remarkable record of 19 years' service, and by the time he quit flying duties in 1941 he had 1174 hours in his logbook. Fornagiari retired in 1950 and lived in Bologna and Lizzano until his death in 1956.

Guglielmo Fornagiari's main awards – two Silver and one Bronze Medals for Military Valour

Guglielmo Fornagiari's victories

Victory	Date	Location	Victim	Notes
1	22/8/17	Ternova	Unknown two-seater	
2	2/10/17	Podmelec	Unknown two-seater	
3	26/12/17	Falzè	German DFW C V, impossible to identify which	With Masiero & Panero
4	26/12/17	Musano	German DFW C V, impossible to identify which	With Comandone
5	27/1/18	San Marino	Albatros D III unknown – *Flik* 55/J	
6	18/2/18	Monte Lisser	Phönix D I 128.08 – *Flik* 39/D	
7	21/2/18		Albatros D III 153.158 – *Flik* 55/J	

Mario Fucini

Mario Fucini was born into a middle class family in Empoli, Tuscany, on 1 February 1891. At 20 he fell in love with aviation when he saw a display by the pioneer airman, Cobianchi. Fucini tried to build a glider from reeds and string, but this only resulted in him suffering a hernia and failing an exam! Fucini would have to wait until 1915 for his first flight following his enrolment in the air service.

His first assignment to a frontline unit came in the spring of 1915 when he was assigned to *25ª Squadriglia.* Fucini duly performed his first operational flights in the unit's Voisins. After a narrow escape on 16 February 1917, when his fuel tank was holed by bullets fired from an attacking fighter and he was forced to glide back over the lines, Fucini declared that he was tired of acting as a target for every enemy soldier on the Isonzo Front. He applied to be a fighter pilot, and after three boring months in a defence flight, Fucini managed to return to combat.

Now with *76ª Squadriglia,* Fucini scored his first victory on 13 November 1917 when he shared in the destruction of a German aircraft with other pilots. Often flying with ace Silvio Scaroni, Fucini scored his

Mario Fucini painted a skull on his aircraft for each of his victories, so this photograph must have been taken on San Luca airfield after his 12th claim on 31 August 1918. Only seven victories were officially confirmed after the war, however. Fucini wears non-regulation cloth overalls, a fur-lined flying helmet and gauntlets

Two American soldiers join their Italian comrades for this photograph. The black squadron number was hard to see on the camouflaged fuselage sides, so it was soon outlined in white. Fucini adopted this insignia before 17 April 1918, when he participated in the fight in which Br C I 229.30 was shot down by his squadronmates. Its pilot, Fw Johan Walenta, described encountering a Hanriot marked with 'a white flag with black spots'. Fucini visited Walenta in hospital, and in the 1960s the two old enemies were put in touch again by aviation historian, Rinaldo D'Ami, after which they exchanged letters second victory on 26 December during the Istrana air battle. His third success came on 28 January 1918 when, over Biadene, he watched in horror as the observer of the enemy aircraft that he had just crippled plummeted to his death. On 11 February Fucini transferred to *78ᵃ Squadriglia*, where he remained for the rest of the war. On 16 June he scored two more victories, avenging Sergente Bocca who had just been shot down and wounded by Ltn Wolfschutz. His seventh, and last, victory was achieved on 31 October near Mandre.

Fucini remained in the air force post-war, having become a full colonel by the time he was granted a special discharge in 1937. He later showed talent as a writer, publishing a book describing his wartime experiences, as well as several articles. Fucini died in Rome on 1 September 1977.

Mario Fucini's main awards – two Silver and one Bronze Medal for Military Valour

Mario Fucini's victories

Victory	Date	Location	Victim	Notes
1	13/11/17	Arcade	Unknown two-seater – *FA (A)* 232	With several airmen
2	26/12/17	Montebelluna	German DFW C V, impossible to identify	With several Italian and Allied airmen
3	28/1/18	Biadene	DFW C V – *FA (A)* 219, Vzfw Max Screiber and Ltn Dietrich Stapefeld both KIA	With Scaroni
4	16/6/18	Pilonetto	Unknown two-seater	
5	16/6/18	Nervesa	Albatros D III 153.222 – *Flik* 41/J	
6	25/7/18	Moriago	Unknown two-seater	With Venier
7	31/8/18	Mandre	Ufag C I 161.107 – *Flik* 22/D	With Chiri & Rennella

Attilio Imolesi

Born in Cesena on 11 October 1890, Attilio Imolesi was working as a car mechanic when Italy entered the war. He volunteered for service with the Army and was sent to Aviano to work on Caproni bombers. Imolesi's application for flying training was accepted in late 1915 and he eventually became a soldato pilota to *Sezione* with *Difesa di Rimini*, this unit being tasked with defending the Italian coast against Austrian seaplane raids.

Although Rimini represented an ideal posting for Imolesi, being just 20 km (12 miles) from his home town, he volunteered for the front, and in November 1916 was assigned to *79ᵃ Squadriglia* as a caporale. On 26 April 1917 he scored his first victory, flying Nieuport 17 2142, whilst participating in a dogfight in which Baracca also shot down a Br C I. A month later on 26 May, Imolesi lost the two-seater he was escorting in cloud over Nabresina, near Trieste, and was hit by anti-aircraft fire. 'I heard a terrible bang, pieces fell off and I felt the aeroplane shake terribly', he later wrote in a letter to his family. The engine died but Imolesi was able to glide back to the Italian coast and crash-land in a swamp.

After a series of inconclusive battles, he scored again on 26 September during a dogfight near Asiago. Shooting down yet another Br C I after driving away an escorting fighter, Imolesi wrote in a letter home;

'In a single bound I was on him. Our aeroplanes almost collided, but remaining resolute, I held down the trigger of my machine gun and hit

A close-up view of Sergente Imolesi in his Nieuport 17. The Bowden cable visible in front of the pilot suggests the presence of a Lewis machine gun on the upper wing, as well as the synchronised Vickers immediately ahead of him. This aircraft could be 2142, which Imolesi used to claim his first victory on 24 April 1917 when he shared in the destruction of a Br C I with Baracca. The fighter's Vickers gun jammed during the course of the engagement. It is possible that the Nieuport's fuselage displays a horseshoe – Imolesi's only known personal insignia

him mortally. I saw him fall headlong in flames and crash in a little square in Asiago.'

Imolesi wrote in his report that the escorting Albatros D III had merely been driven away, but it seems that after the war this aircraft was also added to his score. He claimed his fourth victory after a hard fight on 13 December near Ghertele, and became an ace on 11 January 1918. Imolesi scored again on the 14th near Valstagna, but on 10 March his Nieuport 27 crashed during a low-level flight, probably due to rudder bar failure. Imolesi's head hit the machine gun butt and he was rushed unconscious to Marostica hospital, where he died a short while later.

Attilio Imolesi's main awards – one Silver and one Bronze Medals for Military Valour

Attilio Imolesi's victories

Victory	Date	Location	Victim	Notes
1	26/4/17	Gradisca	Br C I 129.17 – *Flik* 35	With Baracca
2	26/9/17	Asiago	Br C I 129.29 – *Flik* 21/D	
3	26/9/17	Asiago	Albatros D III 53.29 – *Flik* 21	
4	13/12/17	Ghertele	Unknown two-seater	With Ciotti
5	11/1/18	Crosara	Unknown two-seater	With Ciotti
6	14/1/18	Valstagna	Unknown two-seater	With Reali

Giulio Lega

Born in Florence on 12 November 1892, Giulio Lega was a medical student when he was accepted for training as an officer in 1915. His tall stature ensured that he was assigned to the Grenadiers, and while serving with the *2º Reggimento*, Lega distinguished himself in the bloody Italian attacks near Oslavia during the 4th Isonzo battle, as well as in bitter fighting against the *Strafexpedition* in May 1916. Indeed, he was awarded a Bronze Medal for courage shown in hand-to-hand combat near Malga del Costo.

Lega volunteered for the air service in late 1916 and received his wings on 31 January 1917. Returning to the front with *21ª Squadriglia*, he remained a member of this reconnaissance unit until November, when it

On 4 May 1918 Giulio Lega dedicated this photograph to his friend Capitano Alberto De Bernardi, who was CO of *76ª Squadriglia* from November 1917 through to 9 September 1918, when he was promoted to lead *XIII Gruppo*. The Italian Grenadiers, whose insignia marked the fuselage of this Hanriot HD 1, were chosen for their height. They were nicknamed 'extended infantrymen' because of this by other soldiers (*Fotomuseo Panini*)

left the front after the Caporetto retreat. Holding the rank of capitano, and the recipient of a Silver Medal, Lega was selected for fighter training. Having returned to the frontline in early 1918, he was assigned to *76ª Squadriglia* and shot down his first enemy aircraft on 17 March. Lega's second victory was achieved just eight days later. More victories followed during the final Austrian offensive in June, the last of which was shared with fellow aces Scaroni and Ticconi.

After the war Lega completed his medical studies – although he was briefly recalled to duty – and he eventually qualified as a university lecturer. When he died in Rome on 11 July 1973, Lega was also medical consultant to the Italian Parliament.

Giulio Lega's main awards – one Silver and one Bronze Medals for Military Valour

Giulio Lega's victories

Victory	Date	Location	Victim	Notes
1	17/3/18	Col d'Astiago	Unknown fighter	With Censi & Donati
2	25/3/18	Montello	Unknown aircraft	With Fanti & Retinò
3	24/6/18	Onigo	Br C I 369.112 – *Flik* 2/D	
4	25/6/18	Mareno	Albatros D III 153.202 – *Flik* 42/J	
5	25/6/18	Mareno	Unknown fighter	With Scaroni & Ticconi

Alvaro Leonardi

Alvaro Leonardi was born in Terni, in central Italy, on 16 November 1895. Earning his wings at the Cameri flying school in November 1915, he briefly served with an artillery spotting squadron prior to reaching the front in February 1917 with *80ᵃ Squadriglia*, which was based at Aiello airfield.

The unit's Nieuport 11s participated in the 10th Isonzo battle, and Sergente Leonardi scored his first victory on 24 May. That day, several Italian aircraft intercepted an Austrian seaplane patrol from Trieste which was attempting to attack two Royal Navy monitors that were shelling Austrian positions. Leonardi duly shot down a Lohner. He had to wait until 26 October for his second victory, however, and once again it took the form of an enemy seaplane, which crashed near Lake Doberdò under the fire of his Nieuport 17. Leonardi's third kill (a Br C I), on 6 November, was shared with fellow ace Cosimo Damiano Rizzotto during a scramble over San Donà. Leonardi subsequently reported;

'After long and accurate machine gun bursts, the enemy aircraft was hit and immediately entered a steep dive. After more bursts the aircraft crashed in flames near San Michele di Conegliano'.

Leonardi's fourth victory came on 27 November, and his victim was possibly a German Albatros of *Jasta* 1. The official Italian victory list credits Leonardi with eight victories, but it is not clear which of his four claims from 1918 received official confirmation. Those verified probably involved a fighter on 24 March, a two-seater on 23 May, an aircraft described as 'Albatros B 3' on 15 July and a final fighter on 20 August. In October, now Sottotenente Leonardi left the frontline for a period of rest, serving in second-line units.

After the war he returned to Cameri to serve as a civilian instructor at the local flying school. Back in uniform from 1923, Leonardi toured several air bases prior to returning to Cameri in 1934, where he spent the rest of his military career and, indeed, his life. He passed away on 1 January 1955.

Alvaro Leonardi's main awards – two Silver Medals for Military Valour

Alvaro Leonardi waves from the cockpit of his Nieuport 11 (2123) at Aiello airfield, near the Adriatic coast and the ancient Roman city of Aquileia. It was while flying this aircraft that he scored his first victory when he forced an Austro-Hungarian seaplane to ditch on 24 May 1917. Its crew was rescued by an Italian torpedo-boat and taken to Grado. Enjoying a long service career, 2123 was still being used by a local defence flight to protect Naples as late as March 1918 (*Roberto Gentilli*)

In Italy the number 13 is considered lucky, and Leonardi adopted it as his personal insignia. His *80ᵃ Squadriglia* Hanriot HD 1 was also adorned with the unit's 'star of Italy' emblem, simplified in comparison with the version seen on Ancillotto's aircraft on page 15. According to Leonardi's daughter, the number 13 was repeated on the uppersurface of the right wing. This photograph was taken at Marcon, which was home for *80ᵃ Squadriglia* from 8 November 1917 until its disbandment in January 1919 (*Roberto Gentilli*)

Alvaro Leonardi's victories

Victory	Date	Location	Victim	Notes
1	24/5/17	Adriatic Sea	Either L136 seaplane, Freiw Riesner and Fl Gast Plasil both PoW, or L137 seaplane, Stb Maat Hirnickl and Stb M W Wirkner both PoW	
2	26/10/17	Doberdò Lake	K212 seaplane, Frg Ltn M Kramer von Drauberg died of wounds and Flgmr Marcello Anasipoli PoW	With Ancillotto, Cabruna & Lombardi
3	6/11/17	San Michele di Conegliano	Br C I 229.24 – *Flik* 12/D, Zgsf Josef Feiler KIA and Ltn Othmar Schwarzenback died of wounds	With Rizzotto
4	27/11/17	Follina-Zenson	Albatros – *Jasta* 1 tentative identification, Ltn Härtl wound in action	
5	24/3/18	Follina	Albatros D III 153.138 – *Flik* 42/J, Oblt Guido Hauger tentative identification	
6	23/5/18	Fossalta	Aviatik C I 37.56 – *Flik* 22/D, Fw Heinrich Brejla unhurt and Oblt Lázár Illics KIA	With Conelli & Pascoli
7	15/7/18	Unknown	Br C I 429.01 – *Flik* 49/D, Zgsf Franz Pospichtal and Oblt Hans ritter von Becker both unhurt	With Testa
8	20/8/18	Gradenigo	Ufag C I 161.105 – *Flik* 5/F, pilot unknown unhurt and Ltn Ludwig Fisner wounded in action	With Sottani

Carlo 'Francis' Lombardi

Born in Genoa on 21 January 1897 and raised in Vercelli, where his father was a rice producer, Carlo Lombardi preferred to be called Francis, signing himself as such on official documents. His life-long love with aviation began while he was still a child when he attempted to build a glider. When Italy entered the war Lombardi volunteered for flying duties, but he found himself relegated to clerical work instead.

He was eventually able to transfer to flying school, and he received his wings in February 1917, only to find himself far from the front as an instructor. Lombardi asked his mother to use her connections to help him by pulling strings, and he was eventually transferred as a sottotenente to *77ª Squadriglia* in September. The unit soon swapped its Nieuports for SPADs, and Lombardi, now a tenente and nicknamed *'piccinini'* ('kid') by his comrades, scored his first victories during the rout at Caporetto. On 26 October he shared in the destruction of a seaplane with Ancillotto, Cabruna and Leonardi, and two more successes followed the next day near Ranziano, with another two on 3 and 4 November. Lombardi had become an ace in just ten days, he would then have to wait until 15 June 1918 to record his next victory.

Lombardi flew four sorties that day, and it was during the final one that he shot down an enemy fighter near San Biagio. Sources which quote witnesses on the ground noted that his victim was identified by a black band painted around the fuselage. The next day Lombardi claimed a Br C I near Pozzon di Mela, but the onset of poor health prevented him from flying until October, and it is possible that he did not return to the front before war's end. He had flown 295 combat sorties and been credited with eight victories, but only seven can be identified.

The period between the wars represented the golden age of Italian aviation, and Lombardi was among the participants, making long flights to Japan, Africa and Latin America. In 1937 he founded his own aircraft company called AVIA, and produced the L.3 light aircraft in which hundreds of Italian pilots made their first flights – several examples are still flying today. Shortly after World War 2 ended AVIA abandoned aircraft manufacture and turned to producing special versions of Fiat cars. Despite the company going bankrupt in 1976, Lombardi continued to fly, and in 1978 he and the last survivors of *77ª Squadriglia* visited their old airfield at Macron. Three years later Lombardi attended the final reunion of World War 1 air aces in Paris. After an active life, 'Francis' Lombardi died in Vercelli on 5 March 1983.

Sottotenente Carlo 'Francis' Lombardi poses in front of the SPAD VII that he flew so effectively in the autumn of 1917 (*A A A Novara*)

Carlo 'Francis' Lombardi's main awards – three Silver Medals for Military Valour

Carlo 'Francis' Lombardi's victories

Victory	Date	Location	Victim	Notes
1	26/10/17	Doberdò Lake	K212 seaplane, Frg Ltn M Kramer von Drauberg died of wounds, Flgrm Marcello Anasipoli PoW	With Ancillotto, Cabruna & Leonardi
2	27/10/17	Ranziano	Br C I 369.02 – *FIG 1*	
3	27/10/17	Doberdò	Albatros D III unknown – *Flik 42*	
4	3/11/17	Rovarè	DFW C V unknown – unit unknown	
5	4/11/17	Casarsa	Unknown aircraft	
6	15/6/18	San Biagio	Unknown aircraft	Ground witnesses reported seeing 'black band' insignia
7	16/6/18	Pezzan di Melma	Br C I 29.32 – *Flik 41/J*	

Cesare Magistrini

Cesare Magistrini was born on 26 January 1895 in Maggiora, near Novara in northern Italy. He became interested in aviation in 1910 when Geo Chavez crossed the Alps for the first time, despite the pioneer's sad end. After conscription, Magistrini volunteered for flying and was awarded his licence at the Gabardini flying school, finishing third out of 100 students. His desire to become a fighter pilot was fulfilled, and as a

An Italian guard of honour presents arms to honour Oblt Viktor Maly. Magistrini and Nardini (first and third from the right) shot down his Br C I 29.11 on 18 July 1917 and were officially rebuked by their superiors for removing instruments and a gun from the wreck

caporale he was assigned to *78ª Squadriglia* in August 1916. This unit moved to Istrana, near Treviso, shortly after Magistrini's arrival, and it was from here that he began his operational duties by flying patrols and escorts.

In May 1917 Magistrini was temporarily transferred to the Isonzo Front, and it was here that he risked ending his career before it had even started. On the 10th he forgot to 'check his tail' while attacking a two-seater near Mount Podgora, and he was jumped by two enemy fighters. Hit in the back and feeling the blood running down his spine, Magistrini managed to escape and land safely. The wound was not serious, and on 18 July he shared his first confirmed victory with Sergente Nardini when they shot down a Br C I. Later, the two Italian pilots chivalrously attended the funeral of their defeated adversaries.

By this time Baracca had already noted Magistrini's skill, and he asked for him to be transferred to his crack unit. However, the young pilot's CO was not prepared to release him. It was not until November 1917, and after the reorganisation of Italian military aviation following the Caporetto retreat, that Magistrini was able to transfer to the prestigious *91ª Squadriglia*. There, he often flew as Baracca's wingman, scoring his third victory and being wounded for the second time on 23 November when he shot down a DFW C V at low level. Sharing its destruction with Capitano Costantini, he received a bullet in the leg for his trouble and was forced to land his SPAD. Again the wound was slight, but Magistrini was very depressed when he saw the fallen German pilot.

A third wound was sustained on 18 February 1918 when an Austrian patrol attacked a SIA 7b reconnaissance aircraft being escorted by Magistrini and three other Italian fighter pilots. In the ensuing dogfight a bullet grazed Magistrini's right knee, but he was back in the cockpit of his SPAD within six days. On 17 May a chaotic dogfight took place when five SPADs of *91ª Squadriglia,* together with several Hanriots from other units, engaged Albatros D IIIs of *Flik* 61/J that were escorting a Br C I. Ltn Franz Gräser was killed in the flaming wreck of his Albatros 153.221, which crashed near Pero after being attacked by Magistrini.

Magistrini scored his last victory on 12 July, sharing this success with Keller and Scaroni in a combat that put an end to the latter ace's career. After the war Magistrini remained in the air force until 1927, after which he flew as commercial pilot for several airlines. During World War 2 he donned military uniform again and flew hazardous transport missions with the *Regia Aeronautica*, before returning to civilian life post-war. By the time of his death on 26 October 1958, Magistrini had logged about 17,000 flight hours – the equivalent of almost two years in the air.

Cesare Magistrini's main awards – two Silver and one Bronze Medals for Military Valour

Cesare Magistrini's victories

Victory	Date	Location	Victim	Notes
1	18/7/17	Asiago	Br C I 229.11 – *Flik* 24, Kpl Stefan Volosin wounded in action and Oblt Viktor Maly KIA	With Nardini
2	16/10/17	Monte Nero	German two-seater	
3	23/11/17	Cornuda	DFW C V unknown – *FA A* 232	With Costantini
4	7/12/17	San Pietro	Br C I 369.21 – *Flik* 39/D	
5	17/5/18	Pero	Albatros D III 153.221 – *Flik* 61/J, Ltn Franz Gräser KIA	
6	12/7/18	Monte Santo	Unknown fighter	With Keller & Scaroni

Federico Carlo Martinengo

The son of a naval officer, Federico Carlo Martinengo was born in Rome on 18 July 1897. Following in his father's footsteps after completing his classical studies, he joined the *Regia Accademia Navale* in Leghorn in September 1911 and duly distinguished himself as an excellent student. Guardiamarina Martinengo was serving aboard the battleship RN *Dante Alighieri* at the time of Italy's entry into the war, and he soon volunteered for the air service. After training at Taranto, Martinengo was sent to Venice, then Italy's main naval base, in September 1916.

He claimed his first victory on 10 October while flying in FBA 410, piloted by 2º Capo Pietro Valdimiro. Under attack from an Austrian seaplane, Valdimiro managed to position the FBA so that Martinengo could fire above and behind it, knocking out the enemy aircraft's engine. The date of Martinengo's second victory has not been determined with certainty, but it was probably scored on 23 October 1916 in conjunction with French pilot Paul Xavier Garros of *Escadrille* N392.

Martinengo's other victories are well known. On 11 November, and by now a sottotenente di Vascello, Martinengo was transferred to Grado – then the navy's most advanced base – to command the *1ª Squadriglia Idrovolanti*, which was soon renamed *253ª Squadriglia*. During the summer of 1917 he began flying the new Macchi M.5 flying boat and, when enough machines had become available, the *Regia Marina* formed a squadron equipped exclusively with it. Martinengo was assigned to the new unit, *260ª Squadriglia*, during the Caporetto retreat, but its debut was not an auspicious one. On 5 November three outstanding pilots of *Flik* 41/J – Brumowski, Linke-Crawford and Szepessy-Sokoll – shot down the Macchi L.3 escorted by Martinengo and his comrades.

Made CO of the unit in December, two months later he was promoted to tenente di Vascello. In the spring Martinengo returned to his victorious ways during a triumphal day for the Italian naval air service. On 4 May the formation led by Martinengo clashed with a flight of

A small motor boat tows flying boat A78 towards San Andrea Island, location of the Venice seaplane station, shortly after the famous 4 May 1918 action that had brought about its demise. A78's pilot, 20-year-old Hungarian Franz Boros, reported that he had been forced to ditch due to a lack of fuel pressure. After alighting, he tried to find the starting handle in an attempt to either coax the engine back into life or puncture A78's hull and sink it, but he failed and Italian torpedo-boats arrived to capture both him and his seaplane

Martinengo smiles for the camera alongside the wreck of flying boat A91, which was also shot down on 4 May 1918. Martinengo, who was remembered by one of his squadronmates as being a friendly and cheerful young man, was not only a very good pilot, but also an excellent leader of men. He commanded *260ª Squadriglia* from December 1917 until June 1918, and then served as a senior officer in the *Regia Marina* post-war. In his last battle against German vessels on 9 September 1943, Martinengo was killed at the helm of his ship, its bow pointing valiantly towards the enemy (*Roberto Gentilli*)

four seaplanes led by Banfield and a vicious dogfight ensued. The Austrian seaplane A91 alighted and ZwF Boros came down in A78 to find out why. Seeing an Italian seaplane circling above, he attacked it, but the inexperienced Boros forgot to check his tail and was soon the target of Italian tracer fire. A78 was hit several times and was also forced to alight, its pilot being rescued by an Italian torpedo-boat. Banfield too was forced to come down on the sea, but in friendly waters, and he escaped capture.

In June Martinengo left the front after flying 172 combat sorties, the ace being transferred to the Bolsena Flying School, where he also instructed US naval aviators. In September he moved to Otranto, remaining there until the end of the war. Martinengo did not transfer to the *Regia Aeronautica* post-war, choosing instead to remain in the navy. Commanding a cruiser during the Battle of Calabria on 9 July 1940, he was killed in action on 9 September 1943 fighting German ships near the island of Gorgona and was posthumously awarded the *Medaglia d'Oro al Valor Militare*.

Federico Carlo Martinengo's main awards – two Silver Medals for Military Valour

Federico Carlo Martinengo's victories

Victory	Date	Location	Victim	Notes
1	16/10/16	Rovigno	Unknown seaplane	Pilot Valdimiro
2	23/10/16	Caorle	L138 seaplane, Sdkt Franz Viranyi and Stb Masch Wart Hoch killed in action	Pilot Minciotti – shared with Garros of *Escadrille N392*
3	4/5/18	Trieste	A91 seaplane, Ltn Josef Niedermayer PoW	With Calvello, Jannello Pagliacci & Rivieri
4	4/5/18	Trieste	A78 seaplane, ZwF Franz Boros PoW	
5	4/5/18	Trieste	Unknown aircraft	

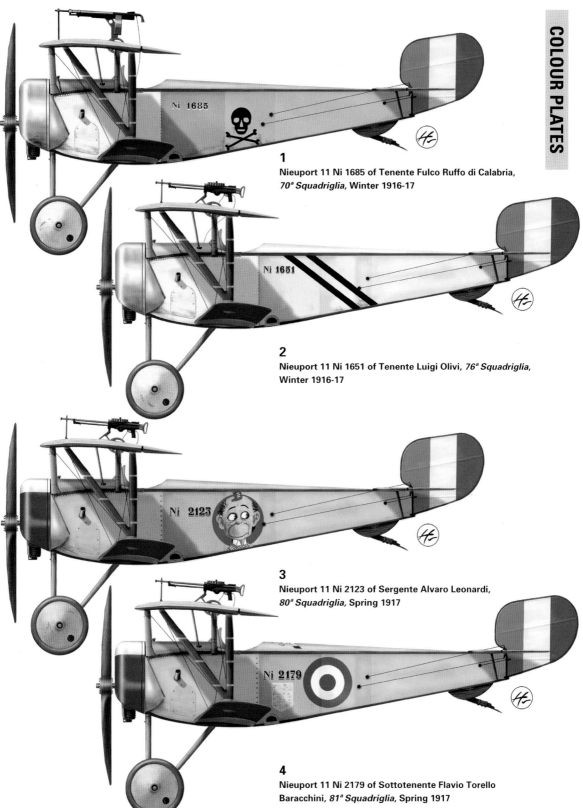

1
Nieuport 11 Ni 1685 of Tenente Fulco Ruffo di Calabria,
70ª Squadriglia, Winter 1916-17

2
Nieuport 11 Ni 1651 of Tenente Luigi Olivi, *76ª Squadriglia*,
Winter 1916-17

3
Nieuport 11 Ni 2123 of Sergente Alvaro Leonardi,
80ª Squadriglia, Spring 1917

4
Nieuport 11 Ni 2179 of Sottotenente Flavio Torello
Baracchini, *81ª Squadriglia*, Spring 1917

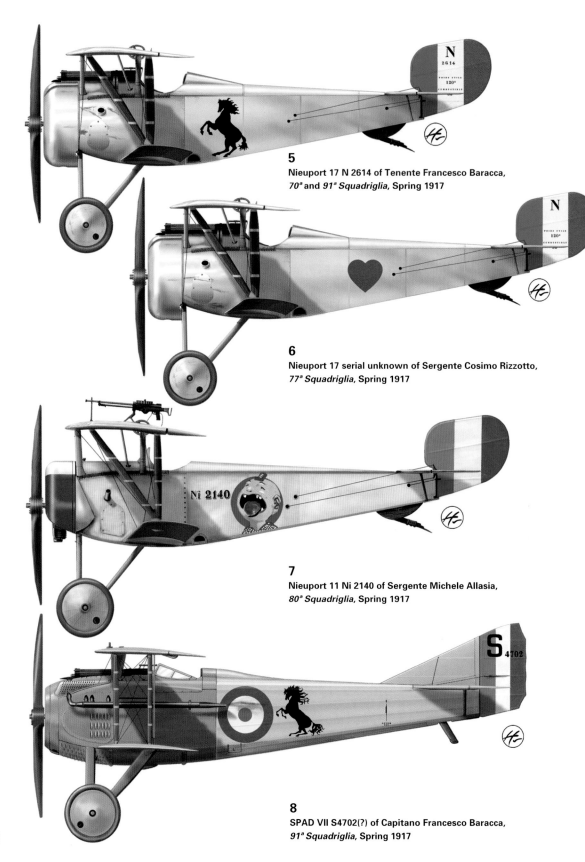

5

Nieuport 17 N 2614 of Tenente Francesco Baracca,
70ª and *91ª Squadriglia*, Spring 1917

6

Nieuport 17 serial unknown of Sergente Cosimo Rizzotto,
77ª Squadriglia, Spring 1917

7

Nieuport 11 Ni 2140 of Sergente Michele Allasia,
80ª Squadriglia, Spring 1917

8

SPAD VII S4702(?) of Capitano Francesco Baracca,
91ª Squadriglia, Spring 1917

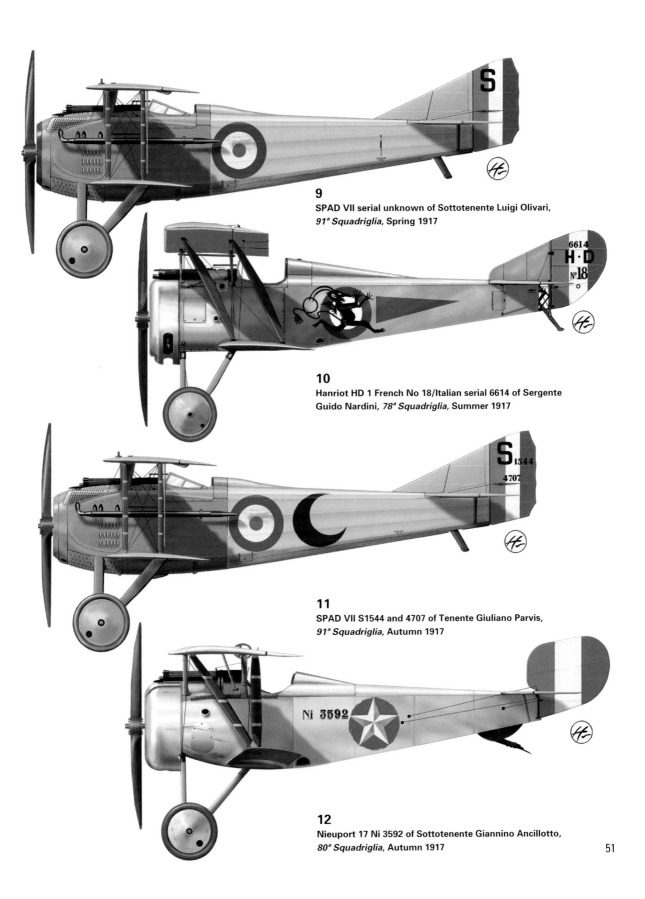

9
SPAD VII serial unknown of Sottotenente Luigi Olivari,
91ª Squadriglia, Spring 1917

10
Hanriot HD 1 French No 18/Italian serial 6614 of Sergente
Guido Nardini, *78ª Squadriglia*, Summer 1917

11
SPAD VII S1544 and 4707 of Tenente Giuliano Parvis,
91ª Squadriglia, Autumn 1917

12
Nieuport 17 Ni 3592 of Sottotenente Giannino Ancillotto,
80ª Squadriglia, Autumn 1917

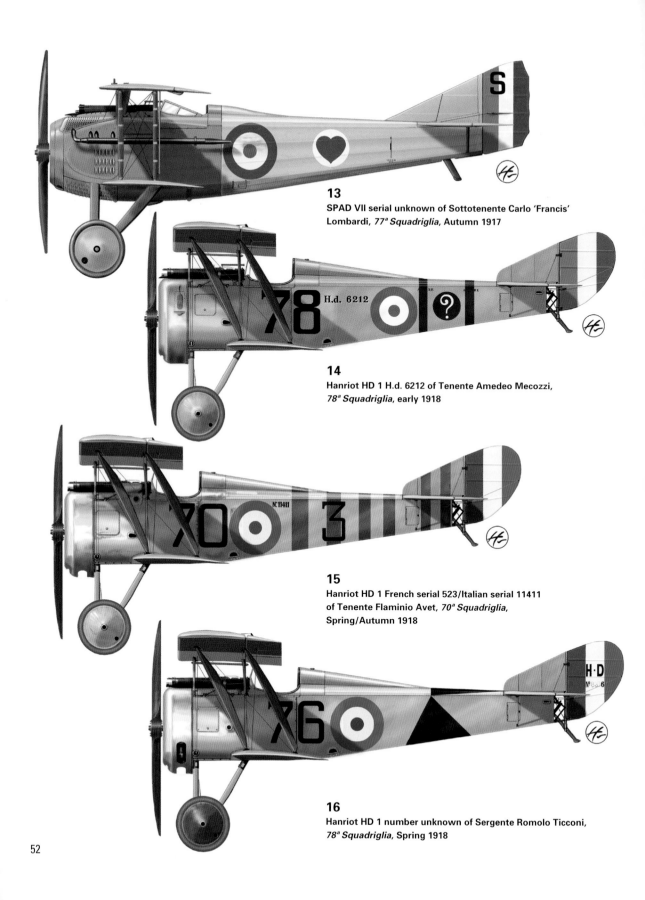

13
SPAD VII serial unknown of Sottotenente Carlo 'Francis'
Lombardi, *77ª Squadriglia*, Autumn 1917

14
Hanriot HD 1 H.d. 6212 of Tenente Amedeo Mecozzi,
78ª Squadriglia, early 1918

15
Hanriot HD 1 French serial 523/Italian serial 11411
of Tenente Flaminio Avet, *70ª Squadriglia*,
Spring/Autumn 1918

16
Hanriot HD 1 number unknown of Sergente Romolo Ticconi,
78ª Squadriglia, Spring 1918

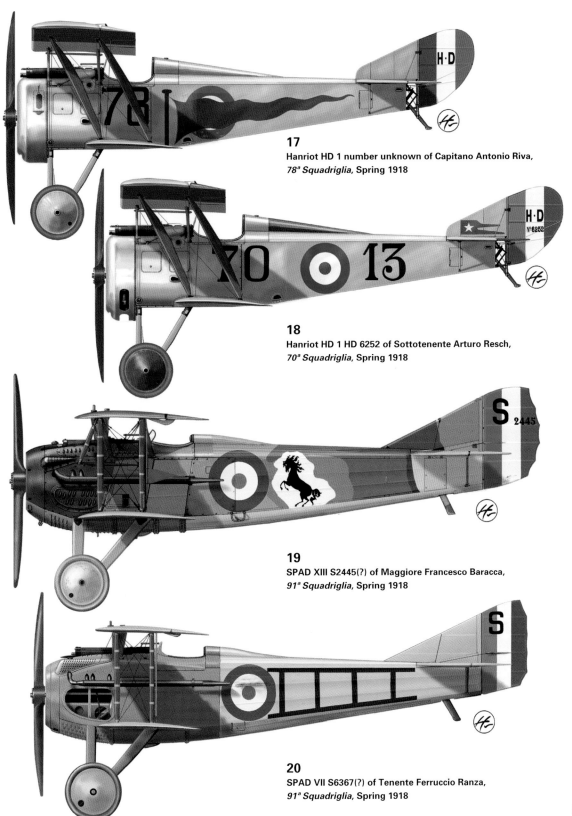

17
Hanriot HD 1 number unknown of Capitano Antonio Riva,
78ª Squadriglia, Spring 1918

18
Hanriot HD 1 HD 6252 of Sottotenente Arturo Resch,
70ª Squadriglia, Spring 1918

19
SPAD XIII S2445(?) of Maggiore Francesco Baracca,
91ª Squadriglia, Spring 1918

20
SPAD VII S6367(?) of Tenente Ferruccio Ranza,
91ª Squadriglia, Spring 1918

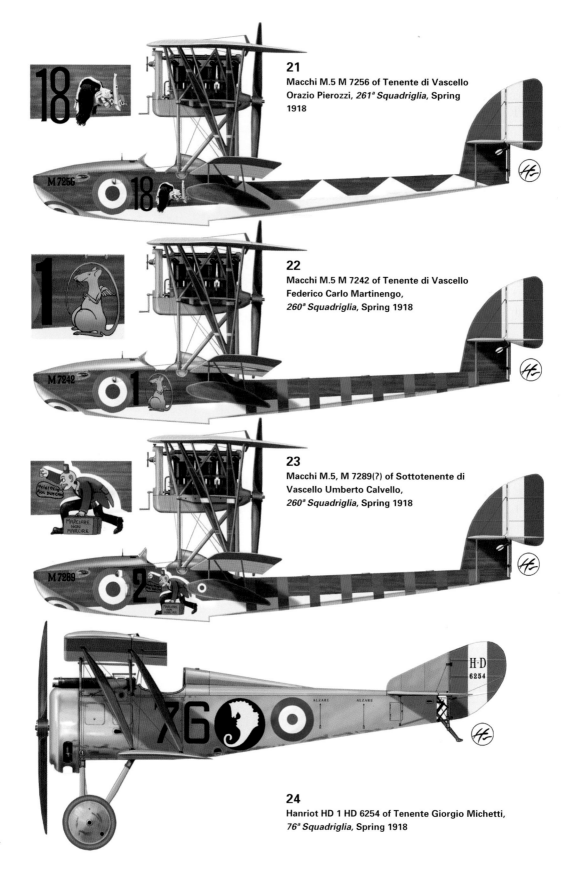

21
Macchi M.5 M 7256 of Tenente di Vascello Orazio Pierozzi, *261ª Squadriglia*, Spring 1918

22
Macchi M.5 M 7242 of Tenente di Vascello Federico Carlo Martinengo, *260ª Squadriglia*, Spring 1918

23
Macchi M.5, M 7289(?) of Sottotenente di Vascello Umberto Calvello, *260ª Squadriglia*, Spring 1918

24
Hanriot HD 1 HD 6254 of Tenente Giorgio Michetti, *76ª Squadriglia*, Spring 1918

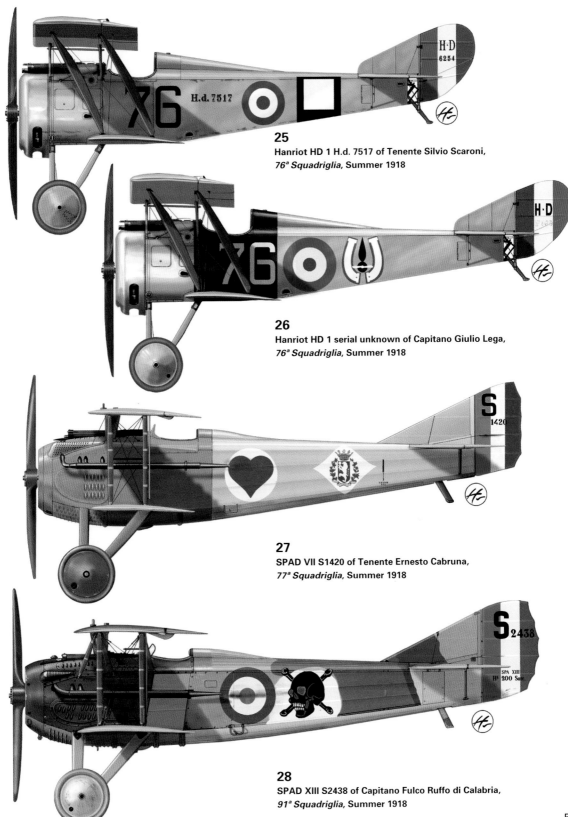

25
Hanriot HD 1 H.d. 7517 of Tenente Silvio Scaroni,
76ª Squadriglia, Summer 1918

26
Hanriot HD 1 serial unknown of Capitano Giulio Lega,
76ª Squadriglia, Summer 1918

27
SPAD VII S1420 of Tenente Ernesto Cabruna,
77ª Squadriglia, Summer 1918

28
SPAD XIII S2438 of Capitano Fulco Ruffo di Calabria,
91ª Squadriglia, Summer 1918

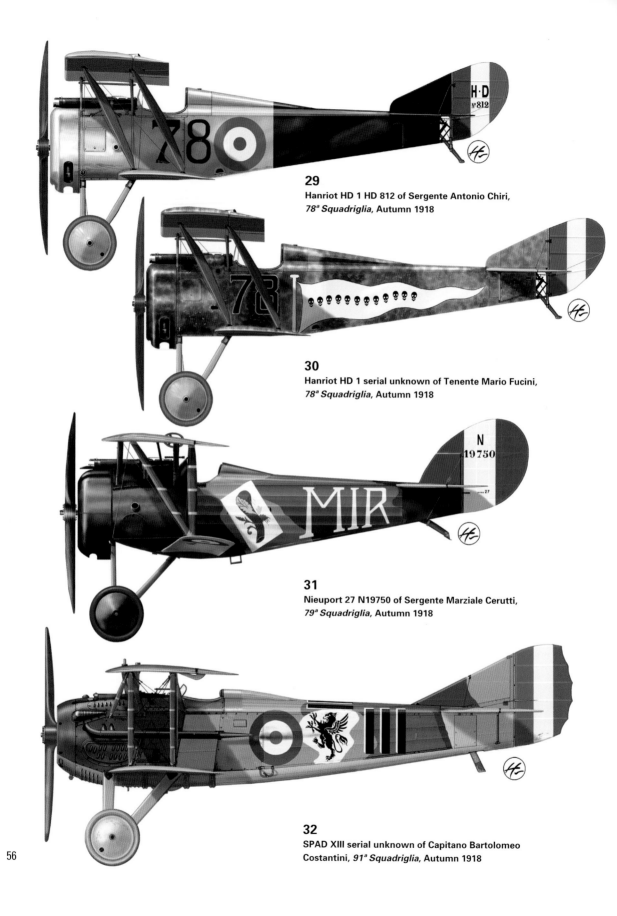

29
Hanriot HD 1 HD 812 of Sergente Antonio Chiri,
78ª Squadriglia, Autumn 1918

30
Hanriot HD 1 serial unknown of Tenente Mario Fucini,
78ª Squadriglia, Autumn 1918

31
Nieuport 27 N19750 of Sergente Marziale Cerutti,
79ª Squadriglia, Autumn 1918

32
SPAD XIII serial unknown of Capitano Bartolomeo
Costantini, *91ª Squadriglia*, Autumn 1918

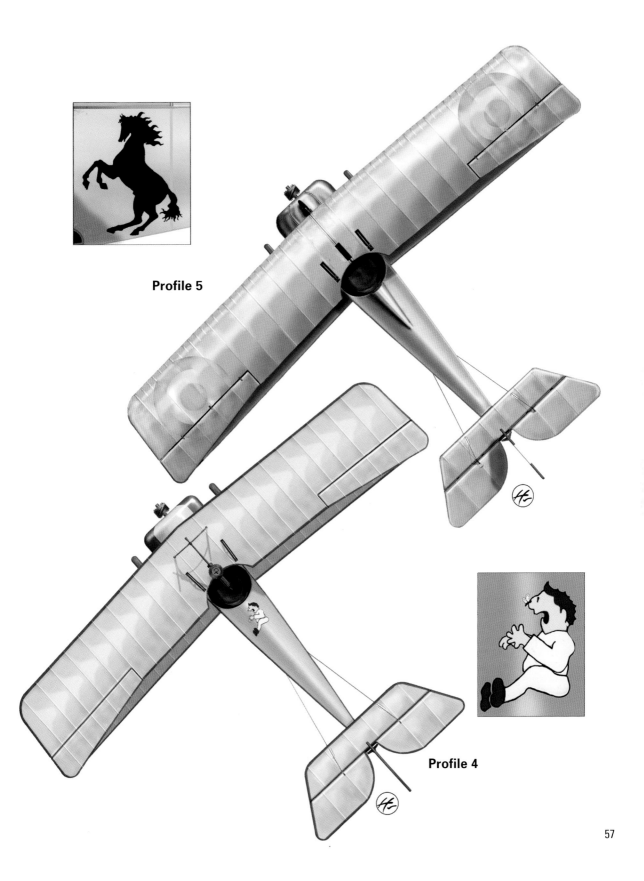

Profile 5

Profile 4

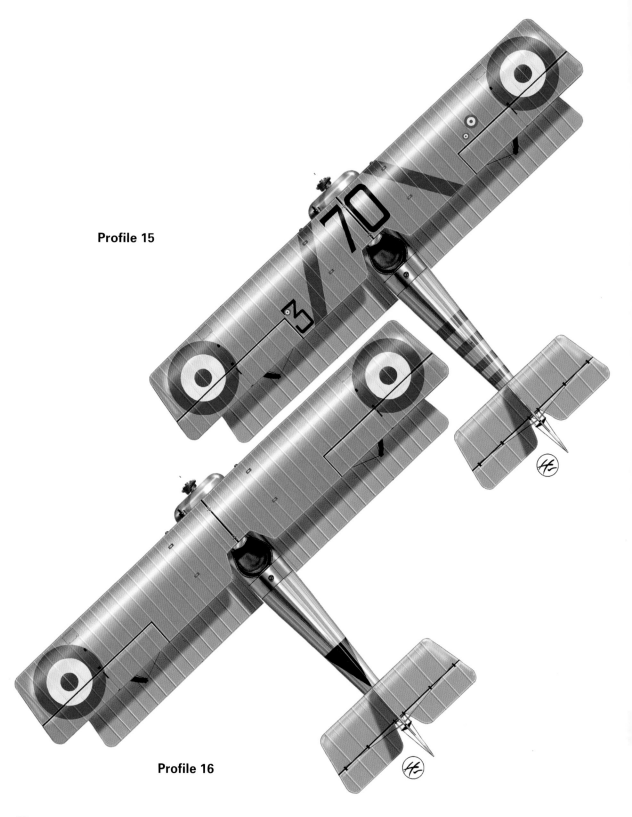

Profile 15

Profile 16

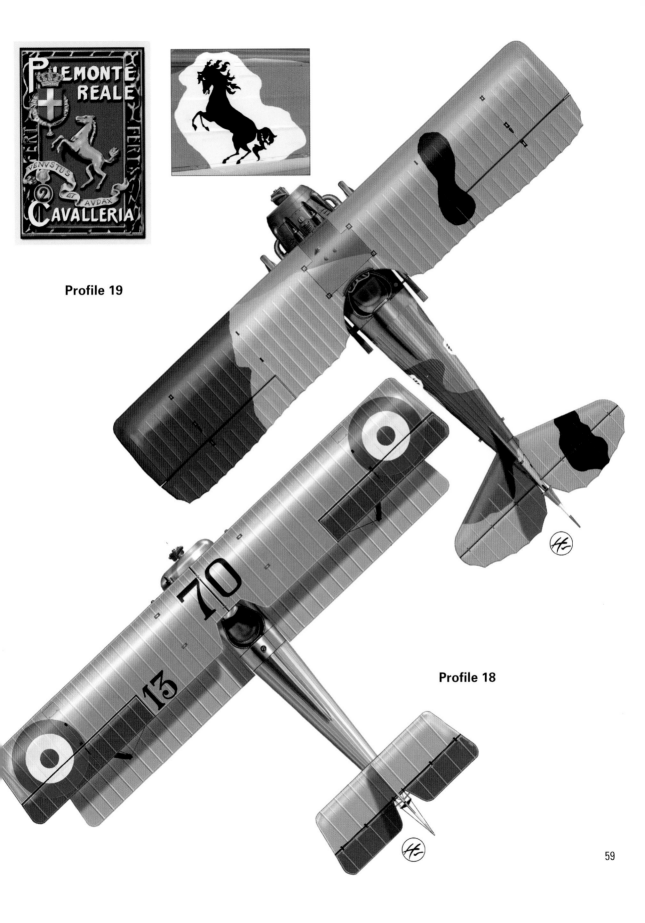

Profile 19

Profile 18

59

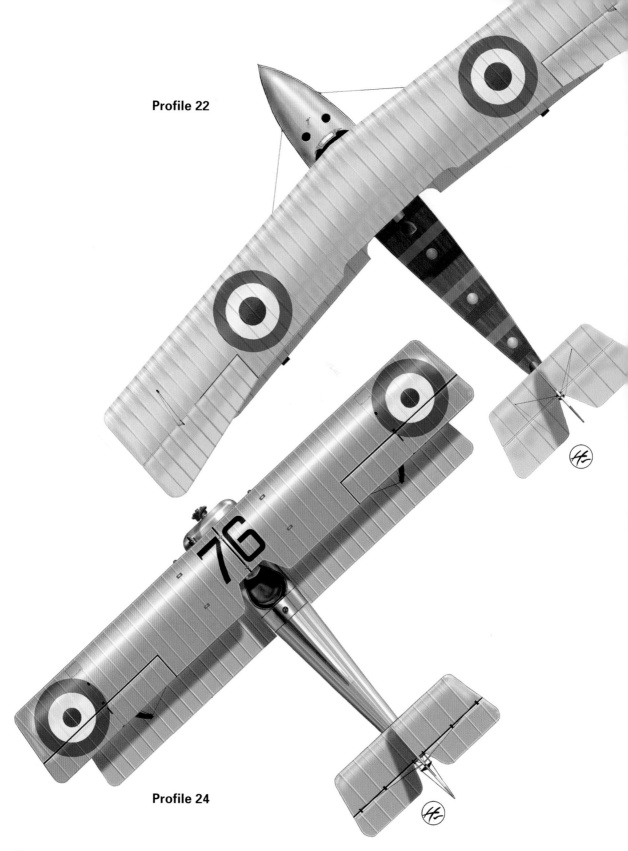

Profile 22

76

Profile 24

Guido Masiero

Born in Padua on 24 August 1895 into a middle class family, Guido Masiero volunteered for the *Lancieri di Novara* Regiment in 1913. Having studied engineering prior to joining the army, he put his technical studies to advantage when subsequently applied for a transfer to flying duties. After receiving his wings, Masiero was sent to *7ª Squadriglia Voisin* at San Maria La Longa in December 1915. Serving with this unit (later renumbered *26ª Squadriglia*), Sergente Masiero flew reconnaissance and bombing missions over the Carso, sometimes returning with his aircraft damaged by enemy fire. The unit was disbanded on 4 March 1917 and Masiero, now a sottotenente with 58 sorties to his credit, was briefly assigned to *103ª Squadriglia* in Brindisi. He then proceeded to the Nieuport training unit at Malpensa and was later transferred to Ponte San Pietro, near Bergamo, to convert to the new SVA. But the situation at Caporetto resulted in all available pilots being recalled to the front, and Masiero arrived there with *78ª Squadriglia* on 2 November 1917.

By 13 November Masiero, together with his friends, Mario Fucini, Chiri and Razzi, shot down a German DFW C V near Arcade. Two more victories followed within a week, on 19 and 20 November, leading to the award of a first *Medaglia d'Argento*. Then, during the triumphal Istrana air battle, Masiero became an ace when he shared in the destruction of two German aircraft with other Italian pilots. This positive trend was confirmed when he was commissioned as a tenente on 17 January 1918.

During this period Masiero met some of the British airmen fighting in Italy. Like other Italian pilots, he appreciated the flying skills of his allies, but contacts were limited by the language barrier and different customs. According to Fucini, Masiero admired the warm and comfortable British flying suits, but would rather have flown in his nightshirt than have 'bacon for breakfast'! On 29 March Masiero left *78ª Squadriglia* for *3ª Sezione SVA* at Isola di Carturo. Despite his best efforts he was not able to increase his score before the war ended, even whilst flying the new SVA.

As his technical and piloting skills were held in high esteem, Masiero was sent to France with the Italian aviation mission post-war, and later participated in the ELTA aeronautical exhibition in Amsterdam. On 14 February 1920 he was one of the select group of pilots who took off from Rome, bound for Tokyo. Of the 11 aircraft that departed, only the SVA of Arturo Ferrarin was able to complete the flight. Masiero was the only other pilot to reach Tokyo, but he had to travel from Delhi to Calcutta by train to collect a spare SVA. Masiero was a member of the air force reserve and returned to active duty for the Ethiopian War in 1935.

In Africa Capitano Masiero flew bombing and ground attack missions in the Romeo Ro.1, Ro.37 and Caproni Ca 101, before returning to Italy in November 1936. In 1937, having adopted the pseudonym 'Guido Magoni', he volunteered for service in the Spanish Civil War, and duly saw combat at the controls of a Breda Ba.65 in the Teruel region. He was now 42 years old and flying alongside pilots young enough to be his sons! Masiero then became chief test pilot for the Breda company and also designed the M.1 and M.2, neither of which were built. When Italy entered the war he volunteered for service once again. Masiero wanted to fly the Junkers Ju 87 dive-bomber in combat, but his work as a test pilot was considered more important and he remained with Breda.

Tenente Guido Masiero is seen here in the summer of 1918 whilst serving with *3ª Sezione SVA* – one of the new strategic reconnaissance units assigned to each army. During his time with this unit Masiero claimed to have shot down a 'red aeroplane' near Trento on 20 May and a fighter over Val Frenzela on 1 July during a leaflet dropping mission. These claims were not confirmed after the war, nor do they match known Austro-Hungarian losses (*Roberto Gentilli*)

After surviving three wars, Masiero was killed during a routine test flight on 24 November 1942 when his Macchi C.202 fighter collided with a second Macchi fighter in thick fog. The pilot of the other C.202, who also perished, was none other than Francesco Agello, who, in 1934, had become the fastest man in the world in his Macchi C.72 racing floatplane.

Guido Masiero's main awards – three Silver Medals for Military Valour

Guido Masiero's victories

Victory	Date	Place	Victim	Notes
1	13/11/17	Arcade	Unknown two-seater – *FA (A)* 232	With Fucini, Chiri & Razzi
2	19/11/17	Vidor	Unknown aircraft – *Jasta* 31	
3	10/12/17	Noventa	Aviatik C I 37.24 – *Flik* 58	
4	26/12/17	Musano	German DFW C V, impossible to identify	With several Italian and Allied airmen
5	26/12/17	Falzè	German DFW C V, impossible to identify	With Fornagiari & Panero

Amedeo Mecozzi's Hanriot HD 1 (6212) is seen here at Nove di Bassano airfield on 26 February 1918. *78ª Squadriglia* had redeployed here ten days earlier from Istrana, which at that time was considered too vulnerable to enemy raids. The unit remained at Nove di Bassano, close to Monte Grappa, until 19 March, when it was assigned to VIII Army and transferred to San Luca. Standing behind the fighter in the black leather jacket is Capitano Antonio Riva, who was squadron CO from 13 October 1917 until 8 December 1918 (*Aeronautica Militare Italiana via Gregory Alegi*)

Amedeo Mecozzi

Amedeo Mecozzi was born in Rome on 17 January 1892 and brought up by his grandparents after the death of his parents. After spending a year as a volunteer in Somalia, he applied for pilot training in 1915 and received his licence on 1 February 1916.

Mecozzi made his first flights over the front as a non-commissioned officer whilst serving with reconnaissance units, and he would often return with his aircraft damaged by enemy fire. On 19 June 1917 he was forced to crash-land his Farman after bullets fired by Fw Julius Kowalczic penetrated his aircraft's radiator. Sent for fighter pilot training in September, Mecozzi, now an officer, returned to the front in October and was assigned to *78ª Squadriglia* the following month. A reflective and studious man, Mecozzi was far from the fighter pilot stereotype, leading his more flamboyant comrades to give him the nickname 'Cato' after the

stern Roman Censor. The jokes were particularly sharp when, on 26 December, Mecozzi shot down his first enemy aircraft and went to examine the wreck near Volpago. He was expecting to be welcomed as hero, but the two-seater had crashed into a barn setting it ablaze and annoying the local farmers. Mecozzi's second and third victories were less problematic, and came in a single mission on the morning of 26 May 1918. Whilst patrolling over Arcade, Mecozzi sighted a two-seater escorted by fighters. He wrote in his combat report;

'I approached them resolutely, followed by sergente Capparucci. I saw them make an about-turn and begin to disperse. I attacked the reconnaissance machine that was nearest, firing about 100 rounds in a single burst. I saw it crash out of control. I could not follow because I was attacking a fighter that was diving towards its own lines. I fired all my remaining ammunition in several bursts, and I followed it until it was about 800 m (860 yrd) from enemy territory. Then I saw it begin to spin, dive straight down and crash into a row of trees near San Michele and Ormelle.'

Mecozzi scored his final two victories on 15 June and 27 July.

Post-war, he remained in the air force and became involved in the debate about its future, eventually developing his own theory of 'assault aviation'. This was often at odds with the strategic role advocated by Giulio Douhet. Mecozzi left the air force after World War 2 with the rank of general, and for some years edited the monthly journal *Rivista Aeronautica*, which was nominally independent but was actually published under the auspices of the Italian Air Force. He used several pen names, but usually adopted *vis polemica*. He also adopted the bizarre habit of wearing a complete flying suit to work! In his final years Mecozzi retreated into silence, refusing to talk about his wartime experiences. He died on 2 November 1971.

Amedeo Mecozzi's main awards – two Silver Medals for Military Valour

Amedeo Mecozzi's victories

Victory	Date	Place	Victim	Notes
1	26/12/17	Volpago	German DFW C V, impossible to identify	With Teobaldi
2	26/5/18	Virago	Unknown two-seater	With Capparucci within Italian lines
3	26/5/18	San Michele	Albatros D III unknown – *Flik* 42/J	
4	15/6/18	Cimadolmo	Br C I – several possibilities as to identity	With Riva
5	27/7/18	Sernaglia	Br C I 169.14 – *Flik* 52/D	

Giorgio Michetti

Francesco Paolo Michetti was a famous painter and a friend of the poet Gabriele d'Annunzio, and his son Giorgio was born in Francavilla, on the Adriatic coast, on 29 May 1888. The latter grew up in an unconventional environment that was dominated by his father's love of progress. After compulsory military service in 1905, Michetti was recalled when Italy entered the war.

Volunteering for flying duties, he was assigned as a sergente to a reconnaissance squadron. In 1917 Michetti completed his fighter training and

Giorgio Michetti perches on the headrest of his Hanriot HD 1 6254 at Casoni airfield, near Bassano del Grappa. During one of the periodical disinfestations of the airfield, Michetti – famous (and feared) among his friends for his jokes – decided to mock the enemy by gathering several rats in a bag and dropping them over Austro-Hungarian trenches. More seriously, he suffered a bad crash at Casoni on 12 March 1918 when his Hanriot rammed an SIA 7b of *22ª Squadriglia* while landing. Both crews escaped almost unhurt, but the aircraft were destroyed (*Roberto Gentilli*)

was transferred as an officer to *76ª Squadriglia* on 29 July. Although he rarely encountered the enemy during this priod, he built up his flying hours on his unit's new Hanriot HD 1s. Michetti was able to put this experience to good use during the Istrana air battle when he scored his first victory. He shared this and his remaining successes with his good friend Scaroni, claiming a second victory on 21 March 1918, his third on 22 May, the fourth on 15 June and his fifth, and last, on 24 June. In September Michetti was posted to the Aerial Gunnery School, and he was still there at war's end.

He and Scaroni visited Argentina in 1919 to promote the sale of Italian aircraft, after which Michetti spent the post-war years in the air force reserve. Little is known about his subsequent life from then until his death in Rome on 4 February 1966.

Giorgio Michetti's main awards – two Silver Medals for Military Valour

Giorgio Michetti's victories

Victory	Date	Location	Victim	Notes
1	26/12/17	Camalò	German DFW C V, impossible to identify	With several Italian and Allied airmen
2	21/3/18	Cascina Zocchi	Albatros D III 153.100 – *Flik* 55/J	With Scaroni
3	22/5/18	Quero	Unknown two-seater	With Scaroni
4	15/6/18	Montello	Unknown fighter	With Scaroni
5	24/6/18	Onigo	Br C I 369.112 – *Flik* 2/D	With Scaroni

Guido Nardini

Born in Florence on 30 July 1881, Guido Nardini learned to fly in France in 1911. The following year, as chief pilot for the Parisian *Navigation Aerienne* company, he became the first Italian to cross the English Channel in an aircraft. When war broke out Nardini returned to Italy and volunteered for the *Battaglione Aviatori*, gaining his military licence in a Bleriot on 1 October 1915.

Despite his age, Soldato Nardini was posted to a combat unit, and on 26 May 1916 was assigned to *75ª Squadriglia* at Tombette airfield, near Verona. Although this city was far from the front, its depots and railway lines attracted Austrian raiders. On 27 June 1916 this allowed Nardini to score his first victory, over an Austrian Br C I from Gardolo, near Trento. He shared the victory with Caporale Consonni and Sottotenenti Buzio and De Bernardi, the two-seater crashing near Arzignano. The four pilots were awarded the *Medaglia di Bronzo al Valor Militare*.

In December 1916 Nardini moved nearer the front when he was assigned to *78ª Squadriglia* at Istrana. It was while serving with this unit that he scored his next victory, on 14 June 1917, when he shot down a Br C I of *Flik* 24. Still flying an old Nieuport 11, Sergente Nardini shared in the destruction of yet another Brandenburg with Magistrini on 18 July. On 6 September Nardini claimed his fourth victory, but was in turn wounded in the thigh by an incendiary bullet. When he returned to the front, his skill earned him a place in the famous *91ª Squadriglia*.

On 10 February 1918 Nardini took off in SPAD VII 6807 for an engine test and, against orders, he strayed from the vicinity of his airfield. When he returned the engine seized and the aircraft flipped over in the ensuing forced landing. This transgression resulted in Nardini being fined 100 Lire – a not inconsiderable sum in those days. He did not take to the SPAD, and was therefore allowed to fly a Nieuport 27 instead. This fighter was not rated highly by other Italian pilots. On 3 May, while flying this Nieuport as wingman for Baracca, Nardini scored his fifth victory. Exactly two weeks

Sergente Nardini, or 'Rigoletto' as his friends called him possibly because of his rather strong features, stands in front of a Nieuport 17 whose serial remains unknown. The aircraft displays the first version of the flag insignia adopted by *78ª Squadriglia*. The photograph was autographed by the pilot on 30 June 1917, 16 days after he scored his first victory, over a Br C I, which crashed in flames on the slopes of Monte Arhentera (*Fotomuseo Panini*)

One of the Hanriot HD 1s flown by Nardini pictured during the last months of the war. Beside the unit's usual flag insignia, this aircraft displays an artistic winged devil cocking a snook at the enemy in a typical Italian gesture (*Fotomuseo Panini*)

later, an Italian patrol encountered Austrian Albatros D IIIs of *Flik* 61/J that were escorting a Br C I over the River Piave between Quero and Ponte alla Priula. Nardini wrote in his combat report;

'At about 1010 hrs I saw a patrol of several enemy aircraft about 200 m (650 ft) above me. Tenente Novelli and Sergente Magistrini, who were at the same altitude as the enemy, engaged a fighter which was trying to evade their attack. It dropped down to my altitude and I attacked him. After some manoeuvres I was able to get into position about 20 m (20 yrd) behind his tail. I fired about 200 machine gun rounds, after which I saw the enemy aircraft catch fire and go into a vertical dive near Pero.'

At almost the same moment the camshaft of his engine broke, forcing Nardini to land in a field near the burning wreck of the Albatros D III in which Austrian ace Ltn Franz Gräser had just crashed to his death.

Nardini finally accepted the SPAD VII shortly after this engagement.

Although he suffered several accidents, Nardini's most serious came while riding a motorcycle on 23 August. Indeed, his injuries were so serious that he was hospitalised until just a few weeks before the conflict came to an end.

In the difficult post-war years, Nardini, like many other airmen, made a living by participating in airshows, but in 1923 he returned to the service and eventually attained the rank of maresciallo di seconda classe. He was killed on 26 January 1928 when his aircraft crashed at Ciampino airfield, near Rome.

Guido Nardini's main awards – two Silver and one Bronze Medals for Military Valour

Guido Nardini's victories

Victory	Date	Location	Victim	Notes
1	27/6/16	Arzignano	Br C I 26.11 – *Flik* 21, Zgsf Josef Holub and Fahn F edler von Langer both wounded	With Buzio, Consonni, & De Bernardi
2	14/6/17	Monte Armentera	Br C I 26.29 – *Flik* 24, Kpl Franz Dostal and Ltn Paul Rotter both KIA	
3	18/7/17	Asiago	Br C I 229.11 – *Flik* 24, Kpl Stefan Volosin wounded and Oblt Viktor Maly KIA	With Magistrini
4	6/9/17	San Gabriele	Unknown aircraft	
5	3/5/18	Salettuol	Br C I 369.28 – *Flik* 19	
6	17/5/18	Pero	Albatros D III 153.221 – *Flik* 61/J, Ltn Franz Gräser KIA	With Novelli

Giovanni Nicelli

Giovanni Nicelli was born in Lugugnano Val d'Arda, near Piacenza, on 27 October 1893. He attended primary school for only four years before becoming an apprentice mechanic. Nicelli was just 18 when he saw the first aircraft to fly over Piacenza, and the following year he volunteered for the air service as a mechanic. After gaining his pilot's licence in January 1917, Nicelli was posted as a caporale to *79ª Squadriglia*, and it was while serving with this unit that he reached the front at Istrana. Promoted to sergente in June, he scored a first probable victory on 25 October 1917, and within the year he was able to add three more to his victory tally.

Giovanni Nicelli (right) and Marziale Cerutti embrace in front of a black cross cut from one of their victims and mounted on a tree. The fabric was possibly removed from the Br C I whose destruction they shared on 5 February 1918. That morning, the two pilots had sighted the two-seater, escorted by a pair of fighters, over the Asiago plateau. They waited until the enemy aircraft had crossed the frontline into Italian territory before Nicelli attacked the Br C I while Cerutti drove the escort away. A report by the recovery unit despatched to salvage the wreckage of the two-seater noted it as having 'dark green uppersurfaces and grey undersurfaces' (*Fotomuseo Panini*)

A further victory was shared with his friend Reali on 30 January 1918 when they sent a two-seater spinning down near Costalunga after it lost a wing. On 5 February Nicelli became an ace when he shot down a Br C I near Case Giraldi, this time shared with Cerutti. On 24 February he and his squadronmates were unable to defend a *26ª Squadriglia* SP that was attacked by Austrian ace Linke-Crawford. In the ensuing melee, Nicelli avenged the SP by shooting down a Phönix.

He scored his last two victories on 4 May while air-testing the engine of his Nieuport 27. Sighting bursts from a nearby anti-aircraft battery, Nicelli flew towards them and spotted a patrol of Albatros D IIIs from *Flik* 68/J overhead the Montello (a hill in the province of Treviso). As he attacked, a handful of British Camels from No 66 Sqn also intercepted the enemy scouts. Oblt Patzelt, flying Albatros D III 153.182, and Kpl Fritsch, in Albatros D III 153.210, both lost their lives in the ensuing dogfight. Fritsch was seen to climb onto the wing of his fighter to avoid the flames and jump clear.

Nicelli is pictured with the tattered remains of one of his last victims, piled up in a courtyard near where it crashed on 4 May 1918. It is not known which of the two Albatros D IIIs shot down that day is pictured here. Less than 24 hours after this photograph was taken, the Italian ace perished in the crash of his Nieuport 27, which, ironically, ended up in another courtyard near Porcellengo (*Roberto Gentilli*)

The following day, Nicelli, a respected aerobatics pilot, was asked by his CO to put on a display for some visiting allied officers. Nicelli took off in his Nieuport 27 11353 and began his display, but as he reached the top of a loop his aircraft lost one of its lower wings. The ace tried to recover by using engine power alone but the aircraft crashed in a courtyard in Porcellengo and he was killed instantly.

Giovanni Nicelli's main awards – three Silver Medals for Military Valour

Giovanni Nicelli's victories

Victory	Date	Location	Victim	Notes
1	25/10/17	Monte Lisser	Unknown two-seater	
2	7/11/17	Fonzaso	Br C I 29.71 – *Flik* 24/F, Zgsf Friedrich Schieg and Ltn Friedrich Wirth both PoW	
3	7/12/17	Val d'Assa	Unknown two-seater	
4	30/1/18	Costalunga	Br C I 29.07 – *Flik* 45/D	With Reali
5	5/2/18	Case Girardi	Br C I 29.16 – *Flik* 45/D	With Cerutti
6	24/2/18	Cismon	Phönix D I	
7	4/5/18	Montello	Albatros D III 153.182 – *Flik* 68/J	With No 66 Sqn
8	4/5/18	Montello	Albatros D III 153.210 – *Flik* 68/J	With No 66 Sqn

Gastone Novelli

The son of an army general, Gastone Novelli was born in Ancona, on the Adriatic coast, on 13 June 1895. He followed in his father's footsteps by choosing a military career, becoming a cavalry officer. But trenches, barbed wire and machine guns ruled out dramatic charges with drawn sabres, and many cavalry officers were assigned to other duties. Novelli was transferred to the 43rd Artillery Regiment.

Still seeking a more exciting military career, yet one which would exploit his passion for technology that he had nurtured since his youth, Novelli volunteered for the aviation service and was assigned as an observer to *11ª Squadriglia*. After 17 missions he put in a request for pilot training, and when he returned to the front on 11 August 1916, he was assigned to *30ª Squadriglia* to fly bombing and reconnaissance missions.

Novelli eventually managed to retrain as a fighter pilot, his first unit in his new role being *81ª Squadriglia*. It was while flying one of its Nieuport 11s that he scored three victories in 19 days starting on 3 June 1917. Two were shared with ace Flavio Torello Baracchini. On 1 August, after returning from a period of leave, Novelli was posted to lead *76ª Squadriglia*. Introduced to the new Hanriot HD 1 at this time, his stay with the unit was to be a brief one, however, for during a

Documents state that Novelli (left) flew SPAD VII S6334 in November 1917, but it is possible that this aircraft was also flown by Tenente Bacula (centre). Some of *81ª Squadriglia's* Nieuports have been pictured displaying playing card insignia, and it is possible that Novelli transferred the ace of clubs from his previous unit to *91ª Squadriglia*. S6334 was subsequently transferred to *71ª Squadriglia*, where it remained until it was passed on to the *1° Magazzino Avanzato* (1st Advanced Depot) in May 1918 (*R Gentilli*)

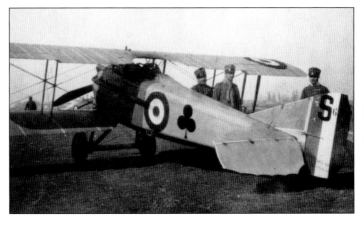

Nardini, Novelli and Magistrini pose with the burned out wreck of Albatros D III 153.221, which they had shot down on the morning of 17 May 1918. The charred body of Austro-Hungarian ace Ltn Franz Gräser was retrieved from the wreck and buried by the Italians in a grave that was never found. For this photograph the Italian pilots borrowed *Arditi* daggers – the *Arditi* were the Italian assault troops during World War 1 (*Aeronautica Militare Italiana*)

reconnaissance mission over enemy territory on 22 August, Novelli was attacked by an enemy fighter and wounded in the left wrist. Managing to cross the lines and land at an Italian airfield, he was rushed off to hospital.

When the Italian Army was forced to retreat after Caporetto, the still convalescent Novelli volunteered for duty and was assigned to the prestigious *91ª Squadriglia*. Flying a SPAD VII, he resumed his victorious ways on 23 November when he and Baracca shared in the destruction of a German Albatros D III from *Jasta* 39. Novelli wrote in his combat record;

'I took off on patrol with Maj Baracca at 1505 hrs. An enemy fighter was spotted over the Montello, and it was attacked by the patrol leader at a height of about 3500 m (11,400 ft). The pilot defended himself, manoeuvring and trying to reach his lines. I entered the fight, firing about 60 rounds. The enemy aircraft crashed into the River Piave, coming to rest upside down on the river bed.'

On the last day of November Novelli gained his fifth victory when he shared in the destruction of an 'Aviatik' with Ranza. The Italian pilots watched it dive 'vertically, without manoeuvring' near Vidor. The first months of 1918 were quiet for Novelli, except for when he was attacked and shot up in error by a British patrol on 17 March.

He encountered the enemy once again whilst leading a patrol between Quero and Ponte della Priula on 17 May. The Italian patrol split in half, and Novelli, followed by his reliable wingman Magistrini, attacked an Albatros fighter. After the Italians opened fire the enemy fighter pilot attempted to escape by diving steeply, but unfortunately for him another Italian fighter – the Nieuport 27 of Sergente Nardini – was waiting at a lower altitude. He set the Albatros ablaze with an accurate burst of fire. Trailing a long plume of black smoke, the fighter crashed near Pero, killing Austrian ace Franz Gräser. Novelli scored his final victory on 11 August when he set Phönix C I 121.26 ablaze near Maserada.

When the war ended in November 1918 Novelli remained with *91ª Squadriglia*, and in early 1919 he was sentenced to ten days in prison after he was spotted performing low-level aerobatics over Parioli racetrack in Rome!

At noon on 3 July 1919 Novelli landed in Padua, having flown from Milan to Zaule, near Trieste, where *91ª Squadriglia* was now based. After refuelling, he took off, but his engine failed immediately. Instead of crash-landing straight ahead, Novelli tried to turn back to the airfield and the SPAD stalled and crashed near a ditch. Novelli, who never wore a helmet, was found unconscious in the wreck. Rushed to hospital, the ace never regained consciousness and died later that same evening.

Gastone Novelli's main awards – three Silver Medals for Military Valour

Gastone Novelli's victories

Victory	Date	Location	Victim	Notes
1	3/6/17		Either Br C I 129.02 – *Flik* 4, Oblt Anton Hoffmann and Oblt Friedrich Wowy both KIA, or Br C I 129.41 – *Flik* 4, crew unknown	
2	19/6/17	Aisovizza	Br C I 29.63 – *Flik* 19	
3	22/6/17	San Marco	Br C I 229.05 – *Flik* 35	
4	23/11/17	Falzè	Albatros D III – *Jasta* 39	With Baracca
5	30/11/17	San Pietro	DFW unknown – *FA A* 232 or *FA* 14	With Ranza
6	17/5/18	Pero	Albatros D III 153.221 – *Flik* 61/J	With Nardini
7	26/5/18	Ronchi	Albatros D III 153.220 – *Flik* 42/J	With Piccio & Keller
8	11/8/18	Maserada	Phönix C I 121.26 – *Flik* 12/Rb	

Luigi Olivari

'Gigi' Olivari, as he was known throughout his life, was born on 29 December 1891 in La Spezia to a middle class family. Keen on sport and all things mechanical, Olivari soon became fascinated with aviation and he gained a civil pilot's licence on 27 November 1914 at Mirafiori, near Turin. Due to a slight heart defect, Olivari was rejected by the army selection board, but after the outbreak of war he volunteered as an aviator and was accepted. He displayed sufficient skill during his military flying course to be included in the small group of Italian airmen sent to France to train on the new Nieuport 11 fighter. He returned in Italy on 28 January 1916 and was posted to *1ª Squadriglia Caccia* in Santa Caterina.

Although still a private soldier, Olivari was welcomed as a friend and equal by Baracca and the unit's other career officers. Baracca scored the first Italian aerial victory on 7 April, but a few minutes later

Soldato pilota Luigi Olivari wore a non-standard flying helmet while flying his Lewis-equipped Nieuport 11. The headgear, shown here, may have been red in colour. In a letter to a friend, written in October 1916, Olivari mentions ordering a red leather helmet from a shop in Turin. Having reached the front as private soldier, Olivari received his commission after a passing an exam in which 'they drove me crazy', according to a letter that he wrote to his mother

Olivari claimed the second when he shot down a Br C I from *Flik* 2 near Udine. On the ground, Olivari displayed a sunny nature and an open smile, and he was well liked. Once in the air, however, he was a lethal fighter pilot who also possessed considerable aerobatic skill. Within five months he had become Italy's first ace, crossing swords on occasion with the Austrian ace Gottfried Banfield.

On 24 May 1917, during the 10th Isonzo battle, Austrian seaplanes attacked the British *Lord Clive* class monitors *Earl of Peterborough* and *Sir Thomas Picton* which were shelling enemy positions. Once the Italian fighter escorts had arrived on the scene, they quickly shot down two Lohners (L136 and L137). The former fell to the guns of Olivari, whose Nieuport 11 received some hits from another seaplane. The Austrian crew later told Olivari that he was very lucky to have survived the combat with Banfield, but the normally shy Olivari retorted sharply, 'He's the luckier of the two'.

His passion for technology had not faded, and on 6 July 1917 (with his tally standing at 11 victories), Olivari was posted to the Ansaldo company to work on the development of Italy's premier fighter, the A.1. On 21 August he rejoined *91ª Squadriglia* and was immediately back in action. However, the stress of continuous combat had taken its toll, prompting

Costantini smokes while he talks to Capitano Guido Tacchini, CO of *91ª Squadriglia*. The pair are standing in front of the early production SPAD VII flown by Olivari, who had its cowling ring painted red. While opponents might not have known Olivari by name, his markings were feared enough to earn him the nickname 'Red Devil'

Lohner L137 smokes before sinking, having been forced to ditch by Olivari or Leonardi in the early morning of 24 May 1917 – the second anniversary of the Italian entry into the war. This photograph was taken from the Italian torpedo-boat which rescued the crew of the flying boat, together with that of L136, which was shot down in the same action. The prisoners were taken ashore suffering from only minor bruises (*Mauro Antonellini*)

Baracca to write that 'His health is very bad and he cannot always fly as much as he would like'. Yet Olivari continued to fight, adding one more victory on 10 September. But time was running out for him.

On 13 October 1917 Olivari left Santa Caterina airfield in his SPAD VII on an escort mission. He was watched by his friend and fellow ace Ferruccio Ranza, who was waiting to take off. Ranza saw the SPAD go into a steep climb and stall in the kind of manoeuvre to be expected of a novice, not a pilot of Olivari's experience. The aircraft crashed, immediately killing the veteran pilot. Baracca, his friend and rival, wrote to Olivari's mother, but the greatest tribute was paid by the enemy. A year after his death, a captured Austrian airman stated that the Italian fighter pilot most feared by his compatriots were Baracca, Baracchini and the 'Red Devil' – a pilot known by the red markings displayed by his aircraft. Olivari's fighters usually boasted a red cowling ring.

Luigi Olivari's main awards – three Silver and two Bronze Medals for Military Valour

Luigi Olivari's victories

Victory	Date	Location	Victim	Notes
1	7/4/16	Udine	Br C I – *Flik* 2	With Tacchini & Bolognesi
2	16/5/16	Gorizia	Lloyd C III 43.65 – *Flik* 2	
3	9/7/16	Salcano	Unknown aircraft	With Stoppani, Venchiaruti & Rigoni
4	25/8/16	Medea	Br C I 64.01 – *Flik* 4	
5	16/9/16	Monte Stol	Lloyd C III – *Flik* 16, Zgsf Franz Morozco and Ltn Anton von Csáby both KIA	With Baracca & Ruffo
6	31/10/16	Val Sava	Br C I 64.14 – *Flik* 16	
7	18/3/17	San Canziano	Br C I 29.53 – *Flik* 23	
8	18/5/17	Vojsciza	Unknown two-seater	
9	24/5/17	Adriatic Sea	L136 seaplane	
10	3/6/17	San Marco	Br C I 129.41 – *Flik* 4, Unknown crew	
11	6/6/17	Vodice	Br C I 229.19 – *FIG* 1, Kpl Alexander Vezsprémy and Ltn Ernst Pirnos both KIA	With Baracchini
12	10/9/17	Biglia	Br C I 329.12 – *Flik* 21/D	

Luigi Olivi

Luigi Olivi was born on 18 November 1894. The son of a *Carabinieri* colonel, he grew up in Ancona and volunteered for the air service as a non-commissioned officer in 1913. In November 1915 Olivi was posted to *2ª Squadriglia per l'Artiglieria*, which was renamed *42ª Squadriglia* on 15 April 1916. He flew as reconnaissance pilot until June of that year, when he left the front for training on the Nieuport 11 scout. He returned to action with *76ª Squadriglia* in August.

On 24 September Tenente Olivi participated in four combats, and his left wing was hit several times during the course of the action. On 3 October Olivi hit back by shooting down a Br C I near Aisovizza. He enjoyed more success on 11 October and on 23 and 25 November. Olivi continued to fly almost daily in all kinds of weather during this period, but he rarely encountered the enemy until the spring, when he became the unit's CO.

Flying one of the new Nieuport 17s, Olivi scored his fifth victory on 28 May 1917 over Mount San Marco, when he shared in the destruction of a Br C I from *Flik* 32 with Piccio. The enemy pilot managed to put some bullets into Olivi's aircraft prior to crashing, however.

Luigi Olivi enjoys a joke during his pre-flight ablutions in a collapsible rubber bathtub at San Maria la Longa airfield. Combat flying involved many risks, but being able to take a bath was a luxury not often enjoyed by those confined to the trenches. Airmen sent home pictures like this to reassure their families, while keeping silent about the other less tranquil aspects of their daily work (*Fotomuseo Panini*)

On 17 June Olivi claimed to have shot down a two-seater which he chased until it crashed behind Austrian lines near Merna. Olivi returned to his airfield and took off again in a SPAD VII in order to take photographs of his wrecked victim. This was possibly his first flight in this type and it ultimately cost him his life. The engine seized after just a few minutes in the air, and Olivi attempted to glide the fighter back to the airfield. The SPAD was heavier than the Nieuport, however, and it stalled, killing him instantly. Olivi had 180 combat sorties in his flight log.

Luigi Olivi's main awards – two Silver Medals for Military Valour

Luigi Olivi's victories

Victory	Date	Location	Victim	Notes
1	3/10/16	Aisovizza	Br C I 68.01 – *Flik* 2, pilot unknown and unhurt, Ltn Leopold Hirth KIA	
2	11/10/16	Biglia	Br C I 61.72 – *Flik* 4, pilot unknown and unhurt, Mg Sch Gustav Weiser wounded	With Stoppani
3	23/11/16	Biglia	Br C I 68.10 – *Flik* 4, Oblt Andreas von Kammerer unhurt and Oblt B G von Hammersberg KIA	
4	25/11/16	Schömpass	Br C I 29.54 – *Flik* 23, Oblt Andreas von Kammerer unhurt and Oblt B G von Gantzstuck KIA	With Ranza
5	28/5/17	Schömpass	Br C I 229.01 – *Flik* 32, Kpl Paul Forgach wounded and Ltn Anton Boeck KIA	With Piccio
6	17/6/17	Merna	Unknown two-seater	

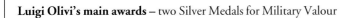

Giuliano Parvis (Giorgio Pessi)

For centuries Trieste represented the crossroads of the Adriatic, a place where cultures and religions met and where Italians, Germans and Slavs lived – and sometime fought – together under the Hapsburg crown. In the 1910 census 190,000 of Trieste's 229,000 inhabitants indicated Italian as their main language, and while there were many loyal subjects of Franz Joseph, many others wished to become subjects of Vittorio

Emanuele III. When it became clear that Italy would join the *Entente* in World War 1, many militant Italian nationalists crossed the border. Among them was Giorgio Pessi.

Born on 17 November 1891 into a wealthy family with strong Italian leanings, Pessi studied engineering and architecture in Vienna and Munich. Once in the country to which he felt he truly belonged, Pessi volunteered for the army, and when war broke out he was serving as a sottotenente. He applied for flying duties, and after training at Malpensa and serving as an instruc-tor for a few months, was posted to a frontline unit. In the meantime, like other expatriates, Pessi was forced to change his name to avoid the death penalty which had been decreed by the Austrians for those declared to be traitors. From then on Giorgio Pessi became Giuliano Parvis.

Giuliano Parvis poses in the cockpit of his uniquely marked SPAD VII in the summer of 1917. Caproni 2386 pilot Tenente Guido Taramelli of *1ª Squadriglia* praised the escort provided by 'the SPAD with the black crescent' in his mission report following a bombing raid of 20 August 1917. Italian fighter pilots routinely escorted vulnerable Caproni bombers throughout the war, regularly fending off enemy scouts during the course of these often dangerous missions (*Fotomuseo Panini*)

When Parvis was temporarily assigned to *91ª Squadriglia* for SPAD training, he was noticed by Baracca, who had him transferred to his crack unit. After several combats Parvis scored his first success on 29 Septem-ber, followed by two more victories on 26 October during the dark days of the Italian retreat. Parvis flew as Baracca's wingman, and the pair claimed two enemy two-seaters, one north of Cividale and the other over Mount Matajur.

On 6 November Parvis 'made ace' when he claimed two victories with Baracca. The Italians had initially encountered two Albatros D IIIs of the renowned *Flik* 41/J near the River Tagliamento, Baracca taking on the leader and Parvis attacking Fw Radames Iskra. After a brief battle Iskra escaped westwards – in fact he had deserted and landed near Treviso – and Parvis joined Baracca. The second Albatros, flown by Oblt Szepessy Sokoll, tried to avoid the Italian fighter by spinning away, but near the ground, when he was forced to fly straight and level, he was hit. With a bullet in his back, Sokoll crash-landed his aircraft but died almost imme-diately. Soon afterwards the Italians engaged a German DFW C V two-seater over Aviano and sent it crashing near Godega.

Parvis scored another victory the following day near Orsago, again with Baracca, but on 23 November he risked raising the victory tally of an Austrian airman rather than his own. That day, accompanied by Tenente Guido Keller, he escorted Caproni bombers on a raid on Feltre. On the way home, the SPAD pilots attacked an enemy Br C I near Mount Grappa, but the Austrian observer was a good shot and damaged Parvis' aircraft. Soon afterwards the Italians were attacked by an enemy patrol from the elite *Flik* 55/J comprising Ltn Lupfer, Zgsf Kasza and Kpl Munczar. After much manoeuvting the Italians disengaged, and upon landing at Istrana Parvis discovered that the Austrian observer had put three bullets into his SPAD that resulted in the aircraft being written off.

Due to a combination of bad weather and leave, Parvis saw no action for several months, and in March he was recalled from the front. After some high-profile executions of PoWs by the Austrians, the Italian Supreme Command had decided to avoid putting former Austrian subjects in positions where they risked being captured. Parvis was sent to the United States instead, where he displayed the Caproni Ca.3 bomber. Indeed, in 1919 he even flew the big biplane under New York's Brooklyn Bridge!

After the war he assumed his real identity once again, and flew for the *Società di Navigazione Aerea Aero Espresso Italiana* carrying passengers in Dornier Wal flying-boats built by CMASA in Italy. On 18 July 1933 Pessi took off from Athens in I-AZEE bound for the island of Rhodes. However, the aircraft flown by the ace with two names, together with his travelling companions, was never seen again.

Giuliano Parvis' main awards – two Silver Medals for Military Valour

Giuliano Parvis' victories

Victory	Date	Location	Victim	Notes
1	29/9/17	Pietra Rossa Lake	Br C I 329.16 – *Flik* 28	With Rizzotto & Sabelli
2	26/10/17	San Lucia di Tolmino	German DFW C V, impossible to identify	With Baracca
3	26/10/17	Matajur	German DFW C V, impossible to identify	With Baracca
4	6/11/17	Fossalta	Albatros D III 153.54 – *Flik* 41, Oblt Rudolf Szepessy-Sokoll KIA	With Baracca
5	6/11/17	Godega	DFW C V – *FA (A)* 219, Vfw Werner Schröder and Ltn Albrecht Binder both KIA	With Baracca
6	7/11/17	Orsago	DFW C V 3955.17 – *FA (A)* 204, Gefr Wilhelm Appelt and Ltn Paul Wilkening both KIA	With Baracca

Pier Ruggero Piccio

A true leader, a 'fire-eater', tough and hard to please, Pier Ruggero Piccio was also brave and fair. He was inclined to disregard rank in pursuit of what he felt to be in the best interests of the service and of his pilots. And Piccio also had a clear vision of the potential of military aviation.

Born near the Coliseum in Rome on 27 September 1880, Piccio studied the classics and attended the Military Academy in Modena, where he attained the rank of sottotenente in 1900. Bored by the dull garrison life, now Tenente Piccio took advantage of an agreement between Italy and Belgium and volunteered for service in the Congo Free State in 1903. After three adventurous years in Africa as a provincial governor he returned to active service in Italy. On his way home Piccio stopped off in Paris, where, during the course of just a few days of celebration, he spent the savings he had accumulated in the previous three years!

In 1908 Piccio left Italy once again to join a multinational force in Crete, which was troubled by factions demanding union with Greece, and in 1911 he fought in the Libyan War. Returning to Italy with a *Medaglia di Bronzo al Valor Militare* on his chest, Piccio was, after many attempts, finally able to fulfil his dream and enter the Cascina Malpensa flying school, where he received his pilot's licence on 27 July 1913. Holding the rank of capitano when Italy entered the war, he was appointed to command *5ª Squadriglia Nieuport* and immediately went into action. The Nieuport monoplane's performance was poor, and the

Pier Ruggo Piccio poses with his rocket-equipped Nieuport 11. His smile could have been prompted by the satisfaction he derived from claiming victory on 18 October 1916. It could also possibly show his amusement at the trick he played on the Venice-based French squadron which supplied him with the Le Prieur rockets that he used to destroy his *Drachen*. These had been given to the future ace on the understanding that they were only to be used in a joint action involving both Italian and French aviators. Strangely, on the day agreed for the action, the normally punctual car that was supposed to take two French pilots to Cascina Farello arrived an hour late, and by the time they reached *77ª Squadriglia's* airfield, Piccio had already taken off! (*Roberto Gentilli*)

unit was disbanded in June 1915. Piccio was subsequently given command of *3ª Squadriglia Caproni* until March 1916, when he was sent to France to train on Nieuport 11 fighters. Once back in Italy, he was posted to *77ª Squadriglia* as CO.

Initially Piccio was disappointed at his lack of success, and he could be heard using particularly strong language when complaining about his bad luck. However, while enemy aircraft remained elusive, the *Drachen* balloons that he now turned his attention to were firmly anchored to the ground. Piccio was able to obtain some Le Prieur rockets, and on 18 October 1916 he used them to destroy a balloon near Mavinhie. This action was quoted in the Italian War Bulletin, and earned Piccio a *Medaglia d'Argento al Valor Militare*. On 15 April, now Maggiore Piccio became CO of *X Gruppo*, reporting directly to the Italian High Command.

Despite being 37 years old, Piccio managed to avoid the dreaded paperwork associated with command to fly combat missions with his friends Baracca and Ruffo. He shot down his first enemy aircraft near Plava on 20 May 1917, and other victories soon followed on the 28th and on 1 June. Then, a double on 29 June made him an ace. By the time German and Austrian troops broke through the front near Caporetto, Tenente Colonnello Piccio had scored 15 victories – he claimed two more on 25 October at the height of the retreat. After the Italian Army stabilised the front along the River Piave, Piccio was able to reorganise the air service in his new role as Inspector of Fighter Units. His commitment to this important task was subsequently recognised by the award of Italy's highest decoration, the *Medaglia d'Oro al Valor Militare*.

Piccio returned to his victorious ways on 26 May when he shared in the destruction of an enemy aircraft with Novelli and Keller of *91ª Squadriglia*, as well as Lt Mitchell of No 28 Sqn.

To face the final Austrian offensive in June, Piccio organised his units in a mass of fighters which immediately gained air superiority. They inflicted significant losses on the *Luftfahrtruppe,* which came to refer to the period as the 'Black Weeks'. During the war's final stage Piccio scored again, on 19 July, when he shot down Ufag C I 161.38, which crashlanded near San Polo di Piave. He described the opposing aircraft as 'fast, very large and with a short fuselage, wings and fuselage *camouflés* like the SPAD, very small crosses and two struts on each side'.

In the autumn Piccio was again commanding the *Massa da Caccia* when the Italian offensive was launched on 24 October. Leading his men into action, on the 31st he was strafing a train near the River Tagliamento when a bullet stopped the engine of his SPAD, 2962. His friend and

wingman Adriano Bacula watched the fighter glide into a field and saw Piccio climb out of the cockpit, at which point he was set upon by Austrian soldiers. When there was no further news of his fate, Italian fighter pilots feared the loss of their irascible, but popular, leader. Then, on the evening of 4 November – the day the Austrian armistice came into effect – a weary and unshaven Piccio arrived at the *91ª Squadriglia* mess wearing an enemy overcoat. Later, over a meal, he told of his capture and how he had been escorted to Villach, where he was able to escape as the empire collapsed.

In 1921 Piccio became Italian air attaché in France. On 25 October 1923 he was appointed Commander General of the *Regia Aeronautica*, the newly-independent Italian air force which had been created the previous March. He was back in France in 1925, but returned to Italy to hold the new office of Chief of Staff between 1 January 1926 and February 1927. On 3 November 1933 the King of Italy named Piccio a senator and two years later he was put on permanent leave after 36 years of duty. He chose to live in France, where he discussed Italian foreign policy with his usual frankness. In 1940 he met his long-standing Belgian friend, and ace, Willy Coppens in Geneva. After they had embraced, Coppens remarked that they were now enemies. However, Piccio showed him a silver cigarette case that he had found in the wreck of an Austrian aircraft and said 'From 1915 to 1918 Italy was at war to eliminate the spiked helmets and now Mussolini has brought them back to us!'

During World War 2 Piccio remained in Switzerland, helping Italian soldiers who sought refuge after the armistice and acting as a mediator between the Italian and French resistance movements. The old warrior died in Rome on 31 July 1965.

Pier Ruggero Piccio's main awards – *Ordine Militare di Savoia*, one Gold, three Silver and one Bronze Medals for Military Valour

Pier Ruggero Piccio is seen here in the cockpit of a SPAD VII displaying the griffon insignia of *91ª Squadriglia*, which began to appear on the fuselages of the unit's aircraft from April 1918. To foster morale after the Italian retreat, Baracca permitted the adoption of a squadron badge to emphasise membership of the crack unit. It was Tenente Guido Keller who suggested the mythical beast, half eagle and half lion, to symbolise strength and excellence both in the air and on the ground

Pier Ruggero Piccio's victories

Victory	Date	Location	Victim	Notes
1	18/10/16	Mavinhie	*Drachen* – BA 12, crew unknown, fate unknown	
2	20/5/17	Aisovizza	Br C I 129.46 – *Flik* 23, Crew unknown, unhurt	With Baracchini
3	28/5/17	Schömpass	Br C I 229.01 – *Flik* 32, Kpl Paul Forgach wounded and Ltn Anton Boeck KIA	With Olivi
4	1/6/17	Staragora	Br C I 29.63 – *Flik* 19, pilot unknown, unhurt	
5	29/6/17	San Marco	Aircraft unknown	
6	29/6/17	Vippacco	Aircraft unknown	
7	28/7/17	Aidussina	Br C I 129.60 – *Flik* 19, crew unknown, unhurt	
8	2/8/17	Tolmino	Br C I 129.? – *Flik* 12	
9	2/8/17	Tolmino	Aviatik C I 37.08 – *Flik* 12	
10	7/9/17	Zagorje	Br C I 29.18 – *Flik* 32/D	
11	14/9/17	Verli	Br C I 229.31 – *Flik* 2/D	
12	23/9/17	Vallone Chiapovano	Br C I 69.44 – *Flik* 2/D	
13	29/9/117	Ternova	Br. C.I 129.44 – *Flik* 12	
14	2/10/17	Bainsizza	Aircraft unknown – *Flik* 2/D	
15	3/10/17	Breg	Br C I 329.20 – *Flik* 53/D	
16	25/10/17	San Marco	Aircraft unknown	With Baracca
17	25/10/17	Castelmonte	Unknown German aircraft	
18	26/5/18	Ronchi	Albatros D III 153.220 – *Flik* 42/J	With Novelli & Keller
19	9/6/18	Moriago	Br C I 269.62 – *Flik* 44/D, pilot unknown, unhurt	
20	19/7/18	San Michele	Ufag C I 161.38 – *Flik* 47/F	
No Credit	29/7/18	Motta di Livenza	Phönix D I 228.50 – *Flik* 37/P	
21	1/8/18	San Polo	Albatros D III 253.40 – *Flik* 56/J	
22	5/8/18	Conegliano	Br C I 369.38 – *Flik* 57/Rb	
23	11/8/18	Maserada	Phönix C I 121.26 – *Flik* 12/Rb	
24	27/10/18	Sacile	Albatros D III 153.162 – *Flik* 101/G	

Orazio Pierozzi

Orazio Pierozzi was born on 8 December 1889 in San Casciano Val di Pesa, in Tuscany. The son of a medical officer, he attended the *Regia Accademia Navale* in Leghorn. During a summer training cruise that took him to New York, he happened to see a flight by Wilbur Wright. On another occasion, according to an unverifiable family story, he met a young and still unknown Manfred von Richthofen in Germany.

When Italy entered the war Pierozzi was serving aboard the battleship R N *Napoli* as a sottotenente di Vascello, and after some further naval assignments he attended the Sesto Calende flying school, where he gained his military licence on 11 November 1916. His initial piloting assignment took him to Brindisi, location of the main Italian base in the lower Adriatic Sea. From here, seaplanes were

Orazio Pierozzi was the leading Italian naval fighter ace of World War 1. Of short stature, he had a distinctive white forelock which is hidden here by his cap. Pierozzi was a staunch believer in the value of high morale, technical training, flight discipline and gunnery practice. He trained the pilots of *260ª* and *261ª Squadriglia* to fly and fight as a team, using a gun camera to improve their shooting skills (*Gregory Alegi*)

deployed to protect convoys shuttling between Italy and Albania, as well as to hunt submarines in the Otranto Channel and defend the Italian coast. Italian flying boats were also often sent to attack targets in Austrian-held Albania, and it was during just such an operation on 30 December 1916 that Durazzo Pierozzi flew his first mission.

On 15 May 1917 the Austrians launched a major attack on Italian anti-submarine drifters and convoys. Pierozzi led two FBAs to bomb Austrian naval units attacking Allied shipping, but he in turn was set upon by a pair of seaplanes. FBA 429, with Pierozzi at the controls and Lombardi di Lomborgo

acting as his observer, exchanged fire with K179. While his Fiat machine gun scored ten hits on the enemy, the Schwarzlose bullets fired by his opponent proved to be more effective and Pierozzi was forced down on the sea. The Italian aircraft had come down between the two opposing naval groups, and it was further damaged by their fire. The crew was rescued by a French destroyer, however. Pierozzi got his revenge on 7 June during an attack on Brindisi when he and gunner Bellingeri finished off K154, which had just been rammed by a Macchi L.3.

On 18 March 1918 Pierozzi was sent to Venice to lead the *Gruppo Idrocaccia,* where he trained his men rigorously in the art of aerial fighting. This commitment soon produced results. On 1 May Pierozzi led three squadronmates in the escort of a Macchi L.3 sent to bomb Trieste. On the way back he attacked the Austrian seaplane A67, forcing it to alight with a dead engine. On the 14th the Venice-based M.5s rushed to defend Italian ships under air attack. In the ensuing battle the Italian fighters claimed to have downed three aircraft, two of which are identified as seaplanes A70 and A85 in Austrian records. Pierozzi's final two victories came on 22 May and 2 July.

Given command of the Trieste Seaplane Station post-war, on 17 March 1919 he was returning to the base from Venice when his aircraft was hit by a gust of 'Bora' wind and hit the water. Pierozzi lost consciousness in the crash, and despite being kept afloat by his fellow crewmember until rescuers arrived, he died the next day. Among the floral tributes at his funeral was a wreath from an unknown Austrian naval airman – possibly his former adversary Gottfried von Banfield.

The Italian word for 'fighter' – meaning a pilot who seeks to shoot down enemy aircraft – is *'cacciatore'* (literally 'hunter' in English). Pierozzi duly painted the head of a hunting dog holding a broken Austrian seaplane in its jaws on the bow of his Macchi M.5. All of the victories that Pierozzi scored during his service with the *Stazione Idrovolanti di Venezia* in 1918 were achieved at the controls of this M.5 (*Roberto Gentilli*)

After the war Pierozzi found a photograph of Seekadett Franz Pichl and pasted it into his personal photo album over a caption expressing respect for the fallen enemy. Pichl lost his life on 14 May 1918 when his seaplane (A85) crashed and capsized off Pola after it had been hit by bullets fired by Pierozzi and other Italian fighter pilots (*Pierozzi Family via Roberto Gentilli*)

Orazio Pierozzi's main awards – Four Silver and one Bronze Medals for Military Valour

Orazio Pierozzi's victories

Victory	Date	Place	Victim	Notes
1	7/6/17	Brindisi	K154 seaplane, Ltn Alois Poljanek and St b Prauer both KIA	Observer Bellingieri. With Daviso & Giannelli
2	1/5/18	Trieste	A67 seaplane, Ltn Josef Niedermayer unhurt	With Burattini, De Riseis & Macchia
3	14/5/18	Pola	A70 seaplane	
4	14/5/18	Pola	A85 seaplane, Seekadett Franz Pichl KIA	
5	14/5/18	Pola	Unknown seaplane	
6	22/5/18	Rovigno	Phönix A115, Flgt Lt Stephan Wollemann wounded	
7	2/7/18	Revedoli	K394 seaplane	

Ferruccio Ranza

Born in Fiorenzuola d'Arda on 9 September 1892, Ferruccio Ranza studied accountancy. In 1914 he attended the first flying training course for officers at the *Battaglione Aviatori* and was then posted briefly to *4ª Squadriglia per l'Artiglieria*. From October 1915 Ranza flew with *3ª Squadriglia per l'Artiglieria*, distinguishing himself for the first time on 1 April 1916 when his Caudron sustained 11 hits by shell splinters.

Ranza managed to get himself transferred to fighter unit *77ª Squadriglia*, and he scored his first victory on 14 September – Italian naval observers confirmed that an enemy seaplane had been forced down on the sea. Ranza scored his second and third confirmed victories during two separate missions on 25 November. In January 1917 he was appointed CO of *77ª Squadriglia*, but by now his skill was now recognised and Ranza was transferred to the new *91ª Squadriglia* on 1 May 1917 – the very day this crack unit was formed around Baracca. On 23 September Ranza scored his fifth victory to become an ace when he shared in the destruction of a Br C I with Sabelli. On 25 October Ranza and Tenente Ferreri attacked an enemy aircraft but were bounced by its escort. Ranza saw three fighters on his wingman's tail as the latter pursued an enemy aircraft. He later reported;

'I saw the bright tracers trails heading for the SPAD, then I saw the latter dive and spin low over the Isonzo towards Tolmino. I didn't see it hit the ground, but I had the impression that the aeroplane was no longer under control.'

Ranza was right. Ferreri's body, buried in Volzana near the wreck of his SPAD, was not recovered until after the war. He had almost certainly fallen victim to German fighter pilot Vfw Münnichow of

The puppy in Ferruccio Ranza's arms growls at the owl perched on the fuselage of SPAD VII S4691. After the death of fellow ace Giovanni Sabelli, Ranza adopted his friend's black ladder insignia (see photograph on page 82), which had been mentioned in the bombing mission report filed by Tenenti Pagliano and Gori on 26 August 1917. Both pilots praised the work of the 'SPAD with the black ladder'. The Italian poet Gabriele d'Annunzio also flew in that action over Lokve as a crewman in a *8ª Squadriglia* bomber (*Fotomuseo Panini*)

Jasta 1, who that same day also accounted for *91ª Squadriglia* ace Giovanni Sabelli. To honour the latter pilot, Ranza adopted his ladder insignia. When the front stabilised after Caporetto on 7 December, Ranza and Sergente Magistrini attacked a two-seater on 7 December. The former reported;

'The enemy aircraft fired a single burst and then started a shallow dive, before turning to the left and then to the right. I attacked it again, flanked by the other SPAD, which

frequently forced me to cease fire to avoid hitting it. The enemy Albatros began to dive more sharply and crashed in flames near San Pietro, between Nove and Cittadella.'

The pilot's charred body was later found among the wreck. The observer had chosen to jump from the burning aircraft.

The year ended for Ranza with his tenth victory, scored on 30 December over an enemy aircraft 'painted in patches of different colours, standing out well against the snow'. The first victory of 1918 was scored when he shot down a German two-seater on 12 January, Ranza flying alone at the time over Padua when he saw the enemy aircraft above him. Unable to reach this altitude, the ace lifted the nose of his SPAD and fired. The German pilot made the fatal error of descending to fight him, as Ranza reported;

'After several bursts the enemy aircraft began to go down in spirals, lightly banked to the left. I saw the enemy observer raising his arms.'

Ranza ceased fire but opened up again at close range when the two-seater straightened up and tried to cross the Piave. Once again the observer decided that jumping from the burning aircraft was the best option as it broke up and fell in pieces near Campo San Pietro. Seeking news of the crew, the Germans dropped a message behind Italian lines containing the missing aircraft's identity – Rumpler C IV 8266/17 of *Reihenbild Zug* 1.

Although there were few combats until spring, Ranza scored a double victory on 10 February. On 15 June (the first day of the final Austrian offensive) Ranza shot down a Br C I. He had few days to enjoy this success, and that of the Italian army in general, because on the 19th his CO and friend Francesco Baracca failed to return from a strafing mission over the Montello. His body was not found until the 24th by Tenente Osnago and Ranza, who carried a white sheet to use as shroud. The war continued, and in September Ranza replaced Ruffo as squadron CO, scoring his last two victories on 29 October. By the Armistice Ranza had logged three years of frontline service, flown 465 combat sorties, made 43 strafing attacks, participated in 57 air combats and scored 17 confirmed victories.

Ranza remained in the army air service and later the *Regia Aeronautica*, adding chevrons to his sleeves and flying again on operations in Libya and East Africa. While other 'top brass' were glad to court Fascist Party officials or plot in the lobbies of the Air Ministry, Ranza was happiest far from Rome and in the air.

According to a letter from ace Bartolomeo Costantini, the wrap-around windscreen fitted to the SPAD VII did not offer sufficient protection for pilots, leading to them suffering from frostbitten faces in winter. To solve the problem, the SPAD in which Ranza is seen here featured an addition to the standard screen, although the ace can clearly be seen still wearing a knitted woollen scarf tightly around his neck

This photograph of Ranza and his SPAD VII was possibly taken at Padua airfield, where *91ª Squadriglia* was based from 1 November 1917. Following an enemy raid on the night of 20/21 February 1918, during which all of its aircraft were damaged or destroyed, the unit moved to Quinto di Treviso on 11 March 1918. The little tricolour cockade barely visible on the trailing edge of the lower left wing covers combat damage. This photo was dedicated by Ranza to Dr Tiscornia, medical officer at Padua airfield, in December 1918 (*Villa Brizza Archive*)

In World War 2, as *Generale di Squadra Aerea*, Ranza held high command during the ill-starred Italian campaign against Greece. When the Italian armistice was announced on 8 September 1943, Ranza was in Bari, in southern Italy. Unlike many of his colleagues and senior officers, he kept cool, working first to avoid the disbanding of Italian troops and German sabotage, then organising collaboration with the Allies to prove that the Italians truly wanted to free their country.

Ferruccio Ranza retired in 1952 and died in Bologna on 25 April 1973. Many older Italian airmen of all ranks still recall and vividly describe the imposing and friendly figure of Generale Ranza, who was noted for his cheerfulness, generosity, skill and courage.

Ferruccio Ranza's main awards – three Silver and two Bronze Medals for Military Valour

Ferruccio Ranza's victories

Victory	Date	Location	Victim	Notes
1	14/9/16	Golfo Panzano	Unknown seaplane	
2	25/11/16	Schömpass	Br C I 29.54 – *Flik* 23, Oblt Andreas von Kammerer unhurt and Oblt B G von Gantzstuck KIA	With Olivi
3	25/11/16	Hermada	Br C I 27.53 – *Flik* 28	
4	23/6/17	Barco	Unknown two-seater	
5	23/9/17	Cotici	Br C I 129.48 – *Flik* 35/D	With Sabelli
6	25/10/17	Lom	German two-seater, unidentified (several possibilities)	
7	21/11/17	Casoni	German two-seater – *Fl Abt* 39	
8	30/11/17	San Pietro	DFW unknown – *FA A* 232 or *FA* 14	With Novelli
9	7/12/17	San Pietro	Br C I 369.21 – *Flik* 39/D	
10	30/12/17	Fonzaso	Unknown two-seater	
11	12/1/18	Campo San Pietro	Rumpler C IV 8266/17 – RHBZ 1	
12	10/2/18	Val dei Signori	Unknown two-seater	
13	10/2/18	Val d'Astico	Br C I 29.68 – *Flik* 17/D	
14	15/6/18	Fagaré	Br C I 269.23 – *Flik* 44/D	
15	16/8/18	San Polo	Unknown two-seater	
16	29/10/18	Oderzo	Unknown fighter	
17	29/10/18	Oderzo	Unknown aircraft (several possibilities)	

Antonio Reali

Antonio Reali was born in small hamlet of Ozegna, in Piedmont, on 31 March 1891. One of many Italians to seek relief from poverty by moving abroad, he worked in Switzerland until he was drafted and forced to return to Italy in 1915. Very little is known of his activities during this period, but it is likely that Reali had acquired some sort of technical skill because he was assigned to the Engineering Corps, from where he volunteered for the air service.

After obtaining his pilot's licence, Reali was sent to Cascina Costa for Nieuport training, being posted to the *79ª Squadriglia* at the front on 13 January 1917. Although he engaged in several combats with Austrian aircraft, and earned the respect of his CO, Reali did not score his first victory until January 1918.

Several months prior to this, he risked ending his career when he almost fell victim to high-scoring Austro-Hungarian ace Frank Linke-Crawford. Ordered to form part of the escort of a *115ª Squadriglia* SAML two-seat reconnaissance machine, Reali and his squadronmates were attacked near Monte Lisser by an Austrian patrol led by Linke-Crawford. The Austrian ace managed to get onto the tail of the SAML, but he was forced to dive when Reali flew between him and his target. The latter was unable to follow Linke-Crawford's Phönix D I because he was immediately attacked by another fighter. Sergente Cerutti then joined the dogfight, despite his gun being jammed. While the battle raged, the riddled SAML was able to flee the area, and all the Nieuport scouts also managed to reach their airfield.

Reali's first victory came on 14 January when he shared in the destruction of a two-seater with Imolesi, the latter crashing in Valstagna. Exactly two weeks later Reali claimed two more victories, followed by a fourth on the 30th and his all important fifth success on 1 February. Reali had waited a year for his first victory, and had then became an ace in less than a month. That spring he routinely flew three or four sorties a day, but he had to wait until June to score again. In the hectic days of the Austrian offensive, activity reached its peak on 22 June, when Reali flew five sorties in a day. There was official confirmation of another victory on the 20th

Pilots of *79ª Squadriglia* are seen here posing in front of their wooden command hut probably at Istrana. Sergente Antonio Reali (second from left with a cigarette in his hand) shared his first victory on 14 January 1918 with Imolesi (extreme left). The other pilots (from left to right) Tenente Federico Comirato, Tenente Umberto Mazzini and Capitano Cesare Bertoletti, CO of *79ª Squadriglia* from 16 June 1917 to Spring 1918. The identity of the pilot at far right remains unknown (*Aeronautica Militare Italiana*)

and a double on the 21st. On 5 July Reali was slightly wounded in the right hand by an explosive bullet fired from the ground, but he was back in the cockpit of his Nieuport the very next day. His aggression led to many combats and claims in the following months, but the strict official confirmation requirements meant that only those claims made on 11 September and 4 October were verified.

After the war Reali returned to civilian life, but routinely took refresher courses as a member of the air force reserve. The Ethiopian War brought him back to active duty, and Reali, who was now an officer, flew the Romeo Ro 1 of *38ª Squadriglia* – a unit he briefly led in November 1936. After World War 2 Reali lived quietly in Como, where he ran an auto electrical repair business. After a serious road accident his sons took him to their house in Fano, on the Adriatic coast, to look after him, but the forgotten ace died of his injuries on 19 January 1975.

Antonio Reali's main awards – one Silver Medal for Military Valour

Antonio Reali's victories

Victory	Date	Location	Victim	Notes
1	14/1/18	Valstagna	Unknown two-seater	With Imolesi
2	28/1/18	Val Ronchi	Unknown fighter	With Cerutti
3	28/1/18	Cima Echele	Br C I 129.31 – *Flik* 21, Zgsf Max Gaderer PoW	
4	30/1/18	Costalunga	Br C I 29.07 – *Flik* 45/D	
5	1/2/18	Cismon	Unknown aircraft	
6	20/6/18	Canareggio	Unknown fighter	With Toffoletti
7	20/6/18	Susegana	Unknown fighter	With Toffoletti
8	21/6/18	Susegana	Unknown two-seater	With Cerutti & Toffoletti
9	21/6/18	Susegana	Unknown two-seater	With Cerutti & Toffoletti
10	11/9/18	Susegana	Unknown aircraft	With Omizzolo
11	4/10/18	Moriago	Unknown fighter	With Eleuteri & Lucentini

Cosimo Rennella

Salvatore Rennella left Secondigliano, a suburb of Naples, in 1892 and emigrated to Ecuador, taking his wife and his little child Cosimo, born on 15 February 1890, with him. Once in Latin America, Salvatore opened a little workshop to service bicycles and Cosimo attended the local schools, working with his father in his spare time but also devoting himself to a number of sports. Falling in love with aviation, Cosimo joined a club that eventually decided to send the promising boy to Europe to learn to fly in 1912, after which he was to return home to promote flying in Ecuador.

After obtaining licences in France and Italy, Rennella returned to Ecuador, where he was welcomed as hero and toured Latin America. His promising career was stopped by the war in Europe, however, for he was recalled to Italy and forced to earn a new military licence, in spite of the fact that he had already obtained one in 1913.

Rennella served at the front as a sergente in various reconnaissance units from April 1916, and after completing fighter training he moved to *78ª Squadriglia* in August 1917. During his early missions he was plagued by mechanical failures and jammed guns, but on 24 September he shot

Italian emigrant and pre-war aviator Cosimo Rennella would survive the conflict with seven victories to his name (*Roberto Gentilli*)

down his first enemy aircraft near Zagorjie. 'Cosme', as he signed himself, using the Spanish translation of his name, was liked by his colleagues, who enjoyed listening to him playing the guitar. He flew often, but only scored his second victory on 21 November, over Mosnigo, followed by two more on 14 and 15 January 1918.

The document listing the official homologation of Rennella's victories is lost, but it seems that six months passed before he obtained his next confirmed score on 20 June over the Montello. That morning there were many dogfights, hard and confused, involving Italian and allied airmen, but it is known that both Brumowski and Hefty returned to their base from those battles with bullet-riddled aircraft. On 31 August Rennella, Fucini and Chiri coordinated their assaults and sent a two-seater crashing into a row of trees near Mandre. Rennella shared his final victory with Cerutti on 27 October near San Polo.

After the war Rennella returned to Latin America, where he flew in several countries and had many adventures. In April 1937 he attended a World War 1 aces gathering in Ohio, but soon after his return to Ecuador he contracted pneumonia and died in Quito military hospital on 3 May.

Cosimo Rennella's main awards – four Silver and one Bronze Medals for Military Valour

Cosimo Rennella's victories

Victory	Date	Location	Victim	Notes
1	24/9/17	Zagorjie	Av. D.I 38.17 – *Flik* 32/D	
2	21/11/17	Mosnigo	Unknown fighter	
3	14/1/18	Val di Pez	Unknown two-seater	
4	15/1/18	Arsiè	Unknown fighter	
5	20/6/18	Montello	Unknown fighter	
6	31/8/18	Mandre	Ufag C.I 161.107 – *Flik* 22/D	With Fucini & Chiri
7	27/10/18	San Polo	Unknown fighter – *Flik* 74/J	With Cerutti

Alessandro Resch

The son of a businessman, Alessandro Resch was born in L'Aquila, in central Italy, on 19 November 1892. Keen on cycling, he was posted to a cyclist *Bersaglieri* battalion after being drafted. Having attained the rank of caporale, Resch became a lorry driver with this unit and volunteered to carry messages to the frontline. On 9 June he saved a wounded officer by bringing him to the rear in his vehicle. Resch fought in the bloody battle near Monfalcone, and after being promoted to sergente, he applied for pilot training. On 8 July 1916 cadet officer Resch joined *26ª Squadriglia*.

While many future aces gained experience in reconnaissance units, Resch was the only one to score a victory while flying a two-seater. On 15 August he was at the controls of a Voisin, having been ordered to bomb Reifenberg railway station with three other aircraft. Once over Komen, the two-seater was attacked from behind by two of the feared Fokker E III Eindeckers. His observer, Sottotenente Lioy, fired two magazines of machine gun ammunition at the first fighter to attack before Resch dived at the other. After emptying two more magazines, one of the Fokkers lost a wing, while the second scout was seen heading for Aidussina. Back at

Tenente Alessandro Resch poses in the cockpit of his Hanriot HD 1 6252, with his *70ª Squadriglia* comrades flanking the fighter's fuselage. The pilot with both of his hands in his pockets is fellow ace Flaminio Avet. It was while flying this aircraft on 22 April 1918 that Resch had a narrow escape when his fuel tank ruptured in flight, soaking both pilot and cockpit. Resch shut the engine down and glided his flying incendiary bomb towards the nearest airfield, but adverse winds forced him to crash-land short of the runway. The machine capsized but Resch was able to escape unhurt. After repair, HD 1 6252 was assigned to the Lonate Pozzolo flying school in August (*Fotomuseo Panini*)

their airfield, the crew counted 30 holes in their Voisin, and filed a report claiming a single victory. Unknown to them, the second Fokker had also crashed, although it must be said that Austrian sources put both losses down to a collision due to unknown causes.

On 22 August Resch was slightly wounded by a splinter, but this was tempered by the awarding of his first *Medaglia d'Argento* shortly afterwards. In May 1917 he left the front for fighter training. Promoted to sottotenente and posted to *70ª Squadriglia*, Resch returned to action in October during the Italian retreat. When German aircraft attacked Istrana, he tried to take-off, but his Hanriot was hit while taxiing and Resch was forced to abandon the attempt. On 17 April he scored his second victory (actually his third), participating in the triumphal triple victory gained over the Piave by *70ª Squadriglia*. On 12 July Resch scored his final victory over an enemy aircraft which, 'after receiving many bursts' he saw fall 'like a dead leaf, leaving occasional smoke trails'.

After being discharged, Resch briefly returned to military service in 1927, after which he was employed by *Aviolinee Italiane*. He continuing to fly civil aircraft during World War 2 and died in Cerchio, near L'Aquila, on 8 January 1966. Resch's son, Arturo, joined the *Aeronautica Militare* and flew the F-86 Sabre with the *Lancieri Neri* aerobatic team.

Alessandro Resch's main awards – one Silver and one Bronze Medals for Military Valour

Alessandro Resch's victories

Victory	Date	Location	Victim	Notes
1	15/8/16	Komen	Fokker E III 03.44 - *Fokkerkampfstaffeln*	
-	15/8/16	Komen	Fokker E III 03.52 - *Fokkerkampfstaffeln*	
2	17/4/18	Valdobbiadene	Br C I 169.35 - *Flik* 52/D	
3	17/4/18	Valdobbiadene	Albatros D III 153.152 – *Flik* 42/J	
4	17/4/18	Valdobbiadene	Albatros D III unknown – *Flik* 42/J	
5	12/7/18	Grappa	Albatros D III 153.259 – *Flik* 30/J, pilot unknown	

Antonio Riva

Antonio Riva was born on 8 April 1896 in Shanghai, China, where his father worked as a wealthy silk merchant. When war broke out in 1914, he was studying law in Florence. Riva volunteered for military service at the end of the year, and in July 1915 he was posted as *sottotenente* to *84ª Reggimento Fanteria.* Once at the front he distinguished himself, being wounded twice and gaining a first *Medaglia d'Argento al Valor Militare.*

In September 1916 Riva's request for a transfer to flying duties was granted, and after receiving his wings he returned to the front in April 1917. He briefly served as a *tenente pilota* with a reconnaissance unit, before learning to fly Nieuport scouts and scoring his first victory with *71ª Squadriglia* on 24 August.

Riva inspired confidence in his senior officers, and on 13 October he was appointed CO of *78ª Squadriglia.* After Caporetto the unit was based at Istrana, and on 26 December it took part in the famous air battle in which Riva gained his second victory. The third came during the afternoon of 27 January 1918 when a *78ª Squadriglia* patrol was escorting an SP two-seater that was intercepted by several fighters from the elite *Flik* 55/J, based at Pergine. During the confused melee that ensued, the high-scoring Austrian ace Ltn Josef Kiss sustained a severe abdominal wound which virtually ended his career and Kpl Gottlieb Munczar was forced to land his damaged Albatros. Some historians credit the downing of Kiss to 2Lt Matthew 'Bunty' Frew of No 28 Sqn, but the Scottish pilot claimed to have shot down an Albatros near Conegliano, far from the scene of this combat. This means that Kiss' most likely victor was either Riva or Fornagiari. Riva scored his fourth victory on 15 June and became an ace the next day when he shot down a two-seater near Fontigo. His final claims came on 28 and 29 October.

Riva briefly remained in the service post-war, acting in a support capacity from Korea during the epic Rome-Tokyo flight. He was eventually discharged and returned to China, where he continued to run the family business. In a recent interview, his son stated that Riva had been introduced to Chiang Kai-shek by Galeazzo Ciano, Mussolini's son-in-law and the Italian Consul in Shanghai, for possible employment as a flying instructor to the fledgling Chinese air force. In 1932 Riva moved to Peking, and remained there even after Mao Zedong took power.

Antonio Riva, photographed here in the cockpit of his war-weary *78ª Squadriglia* Hanriot HD 1, was one of the few Italian pilots who was fluent in English. According to fellow ace Mario Fucini, he often visited British fighter squadrons and hosted exchange visits to his unit by foreign colleagues (*Roberto Gentilli*)

On 27 September 1950 Riva was arrested together with a German and a Japanese citizen. He was accused of being involved in an imaginary plot to kill the Chinese leader using a mortar found in his house, but which was in fact an old war souvenir used as an umbrella stand. After being tried and convicted of 'counter-revolutionary activity', Riva was sentenced to death and shot on 17 August 1951.

Antonio Riva's main awards – one Silver Medal for Military Valour

Antonio Riva's victories

Victory	Date	Location	Victim	Notes
1	24/8/17	Luserna	Albatros D III 53.33 – *Flik* 24	
2	26/12/17	Camalò	German DFW C V, impossible to identify	With several Italian and Allied airmen
3	27/1/17	S. Marino	Albatros D III unknown – *Flik* 55/J	
4	15/6/18	Cimadolmo	Br C I – impossible to identify, several possibilities	With Mecozzi
5	16/6/18	Fontigo	Br C I 369.61 – *Flik* 387D	
6	28/10/18	Vazzole	Br C I 369.70 – *Flik* 35/K	

Cosimo Damiano Rizzotto

Born on 6 June 1893 in Cologna Veneta, Cosimo Damiano Rizzotto had worked as a mechanic pre-war, so when he was conscripted in 1913 he was posted to the air service. Two years later, on 24 May 1915 – the very day on which Italy entered the war – Rizzotto was selected for flying training. He was posted to *77ª Squadriglia* in the summer of 1916.

On 28 February 1917 Rizzotto scored his first success when he forced an enemy aircraft to land near Redipuglia. It was eventually destroyed by artillery fire. On 7 July he scored a second victory near Castagnevizza, writing in his combat report;

'The enemy was taken by surprise and didn't have time to defend himself. After a first burst I saw the aircraft immediately stagger and go down towards Castagnevizza. I didn't leave it until I had used up all my ammunition and after I had seen it sideslip, spin and go into a dive, trailing a long trail of flames and smoke.'

Four days later, on the 11th, Rizzotto had a 'hard fight' over Voiscizza with an enemy fighter which he eventually saw on the ground. After a fourth success, on 29 September, against a two-seater with 'red wheel discs' (an achievement he shared with Parvis and Sabelli), Rizzotto scored his fifth victory – a Br C I – on 6 November. The latter aircraft, shared with Leonardi, was seen to crash near San Michele di Conegliano by Baracca and Parvis. On 15 June 1918 an aircraft described in his combat report as a *'piccolo Brandeburgo'* (little Brandenburg) became Rizzotto's last victim.

Sergente Cosimo Rizzotto spent his entire wartime career with *77ª Squadriglia*, flying almost 500 hours in about 350 combat sorties (*Fotomuseo Panini*)

After the war he went to Latin America and saw combat in the civil war in Paraguay in 1922. In 1935, following a brief stay in Italy, Rizzotto moved to Ethiopia, where he established a farm. In World War 2 Rizzotto was mobilised, but he was captured by the British on 11 April 1941. Returning to Italy in 1946, he worked for the municipal administration of Milan. He died there on 18 February 1963.

Cosimo Rizzotto's main awards – two Silver Medals for Military Valour

Cosimo Rizzotto's victories

Victory	Date	Location	Victim	Notes
1	28/2/17	Monfalcone	Br C I 27.60 – *Flik* 34	
2	7/7/17	Monte Stol	Unknown aircraft	
3	11/7/17	Voiscizza	Unknown fighter	
4	29/9/17	Pietra Rossa Lake	Br C I 329.16 – *Flik* 28	With Parvis & Sabelli
5	6/11/17	San Michele di Conegliano	Br C I 229.24 – *Flik* 12/D, Zgsf Josef Feiler KIA and Ltn Othmar Schwarzenback died of wounds	
6	15/6/18	Grassaga	Unknown two-seater	

Fulco Ruffo di Calabria

The Ruffo family is one of Italy's noblest, having produced many gallant warriors during its long history. Among them was Marquis Paolo who fought in the ranks of the Inniskillin Dragoons at Waterloo. Fulco Ruffo di Calabria, Duke of Guardia Lombarda, Count of Sinopoli, Patrician of Naples and Noble of the Prince of Sicily, was a daring young man who seemed to have come straight out of an adventure story.

Born in Naples on 12 August 1884, Ruffo volunteered for the cavalry after leaving high school. At the end of his military service he went to Africa in search of a more challenging life and worked for a trading company in Somalia, alternating between business, hunting and exploration. By 1914 he was back in Italy trying to raise funds for his own company, but he was recalled to active duty. Ruffo asked to be assigned to the air service, and after attending flying school he and his black servant were assigned first to *4ª Squadriglia d'Artiglieria* and then to *2ª Squadriglia d'Artiglieria*. Having received two *Medaglie di Bronzo* with these units, he then requested a transfer to a fighter squadron. After Nieuport training at Cascina Costa, he was posted to the elite *91ª Squadriglia*. He became a close friend of his commander Baracca, and on 23 August 1916 (less than a month after his arrival), Ruffo scored his first victory when on patrol with the great ace.

In this action Ruffo performed the final part of the attack, but he then had to make a forced landing in his Nieuport 11 when its engine stopped

Veteran Nieuport 11 1685 was still in service when *91ª Squadriglia* was formed on 1 May 1917. The aircraft, pictured here at San Caterina airfield, displays the first version of the insignia chosen by Ruffo. The fighter is unusual in having a Colt machine gun mounted above its upper wing instead of the usual Lewis. Routinely flown by Ruffo during the latter half of 1916, 1685 was also occasionally flown by Baracca. Indeed, Italy's 'ace of aces' scored his all important fifth kill with it on 25 November 1916

after the carburettor iced up. Anxious to save the aircraft from destruction by enemy artillery fire Ruffo, helped by a mechanic from a Farman which had landed in the same field, fixed the fault and flew back to Santa Caterina airfield.

Ruffo and Baracca seemed as much at ease in the air as on the ground, and together they scored further victories on 16 September and on 11 February 1917.

When the unit was issued with SPAD VIIs Ruffo painted a threatening skull and crossbones device

The Nieuport 17 used by Ruffo between December 1916 and April 1917 displayed a new version of his distinctive insignia. Ruffo soon learned that a fundamental rule of air combat was to open fire at point blank range. On 28 February 1917 he was so close to the enemy's tail when he fired that the Austrian crew, after a troubled return and rudderless crash-landing, reported that they had been able to see the black skull insignia on the Nieuport which had rammed their Br C I – mysteriously, Ruffo did not submit a victory claim after this clash. This particular Nieuport 17, serial 2139, later disembarked its Lewis gun and was equipped with just the Vickers, which is missing in this view (*Fotomuseo Panini*)

Baracca and other leading aces of *91ª Squadriglia* had several aircraft available to them at any one time. When the SPAD XIII arrived it was used for high altitude flights, while the SPAD VIIs were reserved for low-level missions. In this photograph, taken at Padua on 20 September 1918 just before a major awards ceremony, Ruffo is seen leaning on the fuselage of his 150 hp SPAD VII fighter, which displays the final version of his personal skull and crossbones insignia. The presence of the griffon on the right side of the fuselage remains unconfirmed

on his new fighter. He continued scoring, gaining his fifth victory on 5 May and his tenth on 20 July. His victory tally grew during the summer, but by then Ruffo was suffering from combat fatigue. In late August, now with 13 victories to his credit, he was granted leave, although he was later admitted to hospital. Ruffo was unable to return to the front until October – just in time for the maelstrom of Caporetto. The months in hospital had failed to blunt his skill, and on 25 October he flew three sorties and shot down three enemy aircraft.

This exploit was followed by a long period of uneventful flying, although he was twice forced to crash land his SPAD due to technical failures. This inactivity lasted until spring 1918, and was only punctuated by the testing of new fighters in Turin and Milan with Baracca and Piccio, as well as the visit of King Albert of Belgium to Quinto di Treviso airfield on 6 February. Ruffo was awarded the Cross of Leopold I at this time. His feelings during this period were disclosed in a letter that Baracca wrote to his mother on 15 May;

'Piccio and Ruffo are furious because for many months they haven't found an Austrian aeroplane to attack.'

Ruffo eventually claimed his 19th victory on 20 May 1918 whilst on patrol with Sergente D'Urso over Nervesa. Flying with the same wingman, Ruffo achieved his final aerial success on 15 June – the first day of the Austrian offensive. D'Urso reported seeing the enemy aircraft 'coming down at full throttle and losing parts of the fuselage'.

After the death of his comrade, and commander, Baracca, Ruffo inherited command of the squadron in the summer while the exhausted Austrians reduced their aviation activity. On 19 September Ruffo handed the unit over to Ranza and assumed leadership of the new *XVII Gruppo*.

On 29 October a punctured fuel tank forced him to land his SPAD in enemy territory, but he managed to escape capture and return to fight again. His friend and senior officer Piccio was less fortunate two days later, and he was seen to abandon his fighter near some Austrian soldiers. When *91ª Squadriglia* moved to La Comina, Ruffo loaded his bicycle into his SPAD and went pedalling off to seek news of his missing superior.

The aristocratic aviator returned to civilian life post-war in order to look after his family. Ruffo duly

became a Senator of the Kingdom of Italy in 1925, and he did not refrain from criticising the Fascist regime, especially after the instigation of the infamous Racial Laws in 1938. After the Italian armistice he collaborated with the Resistance, while his sons fought against the Nazis. One of them, 18-year-old Augusto, died in combat at sea near Pescara. Ruffo remained in touch with his old comrades from *91ª Squadriglia* until his death in Ronchi d'Apuania on 23 August 1946. Thirteen years later his daughter Paola married Albert of Liege and is now Queen of the Belgians.

Fulco Ruffo di Calabria's main awards – Ordine Militare di Savoia, one Gold, two Silver and four Bronze Medals for Military Valour.

This early production Bleriot-built SPAD XIII was flown from Poggio Renatico Depot to *91ª Squadriglia's* airfield on 11 May 1918 by Ruffo himself, and it remained with the unit until 3 July, when Novelli returned it to the depot for an overhaul (*Fotomuseo Panini*)

Fulco Ruffo di Calabria's victories

Victory	Date	Location	Victim	Notes
1	23/8/16	Merna	Br C I 61.61 – *Flik* 19	With Baracca
2	16/9/16	Caporetto	Lloyd 43.74 – *Flik* 16	With Baracca
3	1/1/17	Duino	Br C I 29.79 – *Flik* 4	
4	11/2/17	Orzano	Br C I 27.74 – *Flik* 35	With Baracca
5	5/5/17	Vippacco	Br C I 69.20 – *Flik* 32	
6	10/5/17	Biglia	Unknown fighter	
7	12/5/17	San Marco	Unknown aircraft	
8	13/5/17	Jelenik	Unknown two-seater	
9	26/5/17	Britof	Br C I 126.53 – *Flik* 32	
10	19/6/17	Val d'Astico	Br C I 29.60 – *Flik* 24	
11	24/6/17	Cima 12	Br C I 129.27 – *Flik* 21	
12	14/7/17	Comen	KD 28.43 – *Flik* 35	
13	17/7/17	Log	Unknown fighter	
14	20/7/17	Castagnevizza	KD –*Flik* 42/J	
15	20/7/17	Nova Vas	Br C I 69.84 – *Flik* 23	
16	25/10/17	Lom	Br C I 129.61 – *Flik* 4/d	
17	25/10/17	Tolmino	German DFW, unidentified, several possibilities	With Costantini
18	25/10/17	San Marco	Br C I 29.63 – *Flik* 19/D	
19	20/5/18	Nervesa	Unknown fighter	
20	15/6/18	Grave Papadopoli	Br C I, unidentified, several possibilities	With D'Urso

Giovanni Sabelli

Giovanni Sabelli was born in Naples on 23 September 1886 into a wealthy family whose house enjoyed spectacular views over the bay from Vesuvius to Capri. He studied engineering in New York, and while most air minded Italians earned their licences in France, Sabelli was taught to fly in England – he gained his civilian pilot's licence at Brooklands, in Surrey, on 30 January 1912.

Not only was Sabelli the only Italian ace to learn to fly in Britain, but he was also the only one to gain combat experience before the outbreak of World War 1, having volunteered to fly for Bulgaria against Turkey during the first Balkan War. When Italy entered the European war, Sabelli returned home to enlist in the *Battaglione Aviatori*. Despite his combat experience, and being the holder of a civil licence, he still had to pass new flying exams.

After a short period with the Adriatic defence flight, based at Aviano, followed by Nieuport training in France, Sabelli was finally sent to the front. Assigned to *2ª Squadriglia Caccia*, he had some brief combats but without results. After a short period as a test pilot, Sabelli was selected to lead a fighter flight in Albania in October 1916. This was not the ideal posting for a young pilot keen to score victories, and Sabelli was anxious to return to Italy. He expressed this wish to his friend Francesco Baracca, who was already the rising star of the Italian fighter force. On 23 March 1917 Baracca finally informed him that a transfer was imminent.

When at last he received his long-desired orders in April, Sabelli decided to avoid the risk of their being countermanded in typical military fashion by reaching Italy from Albania in just 22 hours! He travelled by ship from Valona to Brindisi, on the heel of the Italian peninsula, and then by train to Villaverla, in northern Italy, where he rejoined his old unit, now renamed *71ª Squadriglia*. He had been here for just a few days when he received orders to join Baracca, who was busily searching for the

Giovanni Sabelli was sent to Le Bourget, in France, on 15 October 1915 to carry out fighter training on the Nieuport 11, and he did not return to Italy until 1 February 1916 when he was posted to *2ª Squadriglia Caccia* (commanded by Capitano Giorgio Chiaperotti) at Istrana airfield. Sabelli flew his first combat mission from here on 18 February when he escorted Caproni bombers that were returning from a raid on Ljubljana. Sabelli is seen here sat in Nieuport 11 1766, which was among the very first camouflaged aircraft seen on the Italian front. It served with *2ª Squadriglia Caccia*, which was renamed *71ª Squadriglia*, from 15 April 1916 through to February 1917 (*Rozzi*)

best fighter pilots to form *91ª Squadriglia*. Sabelli, whose past experience soon earned him the nickname *il Bulgaro* ('the Bulgarian') chose a black ladder as the insignia to display on his new SPAD.

Sabelli was finally in the right place to show his skill. His first victory came on the evening of 10 August when he and Sergente Michele Allasia shot down a Br C I that was flying long ribbons from its interplane struts near Mount Stol. Sabelli was an impulsive combatant, and on the occasion of his second victory, on 6 September, he and Baracca risked a mid-air collision as they lost sight of the enemy, which force-landed behind Austrian lines. In a little over three months Sabelli had scored five victories, but his days were numbered.

On the morning of 25 October 1917, with enemy troops routing Italian forces at Caporetto, Piccio and Sabelli spotted a two-seater over Bainsizza Plateau. Piccio attacked but was forced to break off when his gun jammed, and his place was taken by his wingman. Sabelli was then targeted from behind by an enemy fighter patrol. Unable to defend his friend, Piccio watched impotently as Sabelli went down, his aircraft trailing a long plume of black smoke. He had probably fallen victim to German pilot Vfw Münnichow of *Jasta* 1, who claimed a SPAD destroyed near Volzana. Sabelli's body was never found, but his insignia flew again on the SPAD VII of his friend, and fellow ace, Ferruccio Ranza.

Giovanni Sabelli's main awards – two Silver Medals for Military Valour

The Sabelli family still owns this caricature of the ace – depicting him as 'The Bulgarian' in oriental dress – which was created by an officer serving with the British Army's 322nd Siege Battery (*Sabelli Family*)

Giovanni Sabelli's victories

Victory	Date	Location	Victim	Notes
1	10/8/17	Monte Stol	Br C I 229.25 – *Flg* 1	With Allasia
2	6/9/17	San Gabriele	Br C I 129.50 – *Flik* 34, Zgsf Stefan Morth wounded and Oblt Bela Gerey KIA	With Baracca
3	17/9/17	San Andrea Gorizia	Br C I 329.17 – *Flik* 34/D	
4	23/9/17	Cotici	Br C I 129.48 – *Flik* 35/D, Zgsf Josef Baier and Oblt Eduard Hafner both KIA	With Ranza
5	29/9/17	Pietra Rossa Lake	Br C I 329.16 – *Flik* 28, Zgsf Andreas Kreidl and Ltn Erich von Luerzer both KIA	With Parvis & Rizzotto

Silvio Scaroni

Silvio Scaroni achieved remarkable results during the eight months he served as a fighter pilot. Indeed, had his frontline career not been stopped by a severe wound, he (and fellow ace Baracchini) could possibly have overhauled Baracca's score.

Scaroni was born in Brescia on 12 May 1893 but he soon lost his father, leaving him and his seven brothers and sisters to help his mother run their seed shop. Scaroni's first exposure to aviation came at the 1909 Brescia airshow, but he had to wait until 1915 to earn his wings. He was serving as an artillery caporalmaggiore at the time when the commander of his training camp asked for volunteers to join the air service.

Scaroni obtained his military pilot's licence in October 1915 and was immediately posted as a sergente to *4ª Squadriglia per l'Artiglieria*. This artillery spotting unit was active on the Isonzo Front, and on 7 November his Caudron G 3 was hit in the engine by shell splinters and forced to land. Scaroni wrote to his mother during this period describing his life at the front;

'We always awake at 0600 hrs, report to the command, which is here in the village, and then get driven to the airfield about two kilometres (1.25 miles) away. From here, according to our orders, we make reconnaissance flights or brief practice flights from the field. At 1100 hrs we go to the village for lunch, returning at 1400 hrs to do the same things. At about 1800 hrs we come back and we are free, but in these villages everybody goes to bed by 1930 so you can imagine what a jolly time we have!'

After the winter pause, activity became hectic again. In January 1917 Scaroni put his free time to advantage by studying for his officer's exam, after which he was assigned to *43ª Squadriglia*, where he befriended Michetti. Together they planned to become fighter pilots. After a narrow escape on 5 May, when his Caudron was badly hit and barely able to get home, Scaroni and Michetti were accepted for fighter training.

During the Caporetto retreat all available pilots were sent to the front, and Scaroni reached Comina airfield on 28 October. There, he was met by Michetti, who had managed to have his old friend posted to the same squadron, *76ª Squadriglia*. In his early missions Scaroni committed typical novice's mistakes, but he survived to finally score his first victory on 14 November while flying a Hanriot HD 1. In less than a month he had become an ace, and on 26 December he claimed three more victories during the Istrana air battle.

In frequent discussions with his groundcrew Scaroni was able to learn how to get the best performance from his aircraft and machine gun. He also studied intelligence reports to determine where the enemy was most likely to be found. This professional attitude produced tangible results, and Scaroni scored his tenth victory on 28 January 1918, his 15th on 22 May and his 20th on 25 June. After the final Austrian offensive, opportunities for encountering the enemy diminished, but Scaroni might still have beaten Baracca's record if a bullet fired by Josef Vratil of *Flik* 14/J on 12 July had not almost killed him.

That day he had joined two British Camels in a dogfight with several Austrian fighters and shot two of the latter down. These successes were later confirmed by Lts Rice-Oxley and Howell of No 45 Sqn. In the middle of the engagement Scaroni suddenly found himself alone, although he soon saw an enemy aircraft flying above him. Fixated with the latter, he made the almost-fatal mistake of not checking his tail and his aircraft was riddled with bullets, one of which hit him in the back. Scaroni fainted, then

Italian and British soldiers gather round one of two German DFW C Vs shot down by Silvio Scaroni on the morning of 26 December 1917 during the great Istrana air battle. When the alarm was sounded that morning, Scaroni sighted the incoming enemy aircraft through binoculars and quickly took off. He attacked the nearest machine in the first patrol while bombs were exploding on his airfield, the DFW's crew apparently being too busy with its strafing attack to notice the Hanriot HD 1 bearing down on them. After just two bursts Scaroni saw the C V crash, followed soon afterwards by a second two-seater. A few hours later he downed a third aircraft from the second wave that attacked Istrana at around midday (*Aeronautica Militare Italiana*)

Scaroni (left) poses with his trusty armourer, Luigi Botter, at Casoni airfield in the early summer of 1918. In his book Scaroni credits much of his success to his groundcrew, engine mechanic 'Toni' and Botter, who was nicknamed 'Bigio' ('dark man' in Italian). The latter helped Scaroni to check his ammunition, discarding about 70 per cent of the rounds as defective. He also ensured that the fighter's gun was correctly sighted on the firing range (*Bernardo Sclerandi*)

regained consciousness long enough to crash-land his fighter. Rushed to hospital, he was fortunate to survive. Subsequently awarded the *Medaglia d'Oro al Valor Militare*, Scaroni's war was over and his victory list stopped at 26 – just eight fewer than Baracca.

Scaroni stayed in the air force post-war, rising through the ranks of the *Regia Aeronautica*. He served in such prestigious postings as Air Attaché in Washington, DC, Aide de Camp to King Vittorio Emanuele III and chief of the Italian Aviation Mission in China. During World War 2 Generale Scaroni commanded the Italian air forces in Sicily. After the armistice he retired to his house in Carzago della Riviera on Lake Garda. It was here on 16 February 1977 that Italy's second highest-scoring ace of the Great War died.

Silvio Scaroni's main awards – one Gold, two Silver and one Bronze Medals for Military Valour

Hanriot HD 1 7517's frontline career came to an abrupt end on 12 July 1918. Scaroni, having been severely wounded in the stomach, regained consciousness at about 2400 ft after hitting his head against the struts of his aircraft. He was able to muster sufficient strength to cross the River Piave, at which point the engine of his fighter blew up and destroyed the cowling. Scaroni hastily crash-landed the Hanriot in the only spot available – a dry river bed near Monte Grappa. The wheels hit a hole in the ground, causing the tail to lift and throwing Scaroni from the cockpit (*Fotomuseo Panini*)

Silvio Scaroni's victories

Victory	Date	Place	Victim	Notes
1	14/11/17	Colbertaldo	Unknown aircraft	
2	18/11/17	San Donà	Unknown aircraft – *Jasta* 1	
3	19/11/17	Vidor	Unknown aircraft – *Jasta* 31	
4	5/12/17	Onigo	Aviatik C I 114.12 – *Flik* 53/D	
5	10/12/17	Noventa	Aviatik C I 37.24 – *Flik* 58	
6	26/12/17	Musano	German DFW C V, impossible to identify	With several Italian and Allied airmen
7	26/12/17	Camalò	German DFW C V, Impossible to identify	With several Italian and Allied airmen
8	26/12/17	Biadene	AEG G IV – *Boghol* 4	
9	14/1/18	Valbella	Br D I 28.71 – *Flik* 21/D	
10	28/1/18	Biadene	DFW C V – *FA (A)* 219, Vfw ax Screiber and Ltn Dietrich Stapefeld both KIA	With Fucini
11	11/2/18	Grigno	Aviatik C.I 137.20 – *Flik* 101/G	
12	11/2/18	Fontanasecca	Phönix D I 328.18 – *Flik* 8/D	
13	18/2/18	Pederobba	Unknown two-seater	Within Italian lines
14	21/3/18	Cascina Zocchi	Albatros D III 153.100 – *Flik* 55/J	With Michetti
15	22/5/18	Quero	Unknown two-seater	With Michetti
16	8/6/18	Cismon	Br C I 369.40 – *Flik* 11/F	
17	15/6/18	Montello	Unknown fighter	With Michetti
18	21/6/18	Mandre	Aviatik D I 115.31 – *Flik* 68/J	
19	24/6/18	Onigo	Br C I 369.112 – *Flik* 2/D	With Michetti
20	25/6/18	Mareno	Albatros D III 153.202 – *Flik* 42/J	
21	25/6/18	Mareno	Unknown fighter	With Lega & Ticconi
22	7/7/18	Valbella	Br C I 169.68 – *Flik* 45/D	With Ticconi
23	7/7/18	Valbella	Albatros D III 153.240 – *Flik* 9/J	
24	7/7/18	Casoni	Phönix D I 128.19 – *Flik* 14/J	
25	12/7/18	Monte Santo	Unknown fighter	With Keller & Magistrini
26	12/7/18	Monte Tomatico	Albatros D III 153.259 – *Flik* 30/J, pilot unknown and unhurt	With Howell & Rice-Oxley

Mario Stoppani

Mario Stoppani was born on 24 May 1895 in Lovere. He enlisted in the air service when he was just 18 years old and worked as a motor mechanic. Italy entered the war on his 20th birthday, and Stoppani, who had earned his pilot's licence in February 1915, briefly served with an artillery spotting squadron and as an instructor. In May 1916 he was posted to *76ª Squadriglia* at La Comina, and after scoring his first victory on 9 July he achieved two more during the summer, followed by a further three successes between October-December.

In addition to being a dedicated fighter pilot, capable of gaining six victories in a few months of infrequent encounters with the enemy, Stoppani was also able to find time for

Sergente Stoppani is seen here in his Nieuport 11, operated by the *Terza Sezione* (Third Section) of *76ª Squadriglia*. This photograph was possibly taken in the winter of 1916-17 at San Maria la Longa or Borgnano, just prior to Stoppani being posted to the *Direzione Tecnica dell'Aviazione Militare* (Technical Directorate of the Military Aviation) as a test pilot. The rear element of the rudimentary aiming device – a simple indented plate on the windscreen – is noteworthy (*Aeronautica Militare Italiana*)

other energetic pursuits. The local parish priest once named him publicly during Mass, warning local girls to avoid this 'messenger of the Devil'! According to Fucini, Stoppani, despite many warnings, had removed the lightning conductor from the church steeple with his aircraft. He was reprimanded by his CO, but remained proud of his feat which had left the undercarriage of his Nieuport damaged but the propeller intact.

A pilot with such flying skill could not remain unnoticed, and Stoppani soon left the front to work at the Ansaldo factory on the development of the SVA fighter. He was not to return to the front. While this obviously prevented him from gaining further victories, it resulted in a long career of test and record flying, which continued after the Armistice, through World War 2 and into the 1950s. After leaving Ansaldo, Stoppani worked for CRDA, breaking several world records during the 1930s while flying Cant Z.501 and Z.506 seaplanes. Later working for Breda and SIAI Marchetti, Stoppani died suddenly on 20 September 1959 just one week after his last flight in a Nardi FN.333 amphibian.

Mario Stoppani's main awards – two Silver Medals for Military Valour

Italian infantry soldiers gather round the wreck of Stoppani's fifth victim – a victory he shared with other pilots – on 31 October 1916 near Nad Logem. The gunner, Zgsf Gustav Resch (no relation to the Italian ace), had been wounded and was taken to hospital, while the pilot, Oblt Franz Cik, who died during the combat, was buried on the spot by an Italian military chaplain (*Mauro Antonellini*)

Mario Stoppani's victories

Victory	Date	Location	Victim	Notes
1	9/7/16	Salcano	Unknown aircraft	With Venchiaruti & Rigoni
2	18/7/16	San Marco	Lloyd C III 43.83 – *Flik* 4, Zgsf Josef Franke and Ltn Johann Kiss both unhurt	
3	13/8/16	Ranziano	Unknown aircraft	
4	11/10/16	Biglia	Br C I 61.72 – *Flik* 4, pilot unknown unhurt and Mg Sch Gustav Weiser wounded	
5	31/10/16	Nad Logem	Br C I 68.25 – *Flik* 12, Zgsf Gustav Resch wounded and Oblt Franz Cik KIA	Shared with other pilots
6	1/12/16	San Marco	Unknown aircraft	

Romolo Ticconi

Born in Acuto on 25 March 1893, Romolo Ticconi grew up in Rome and was working as a stonemason when he was drafted in August 1915. After service with an infantry regiment he was accepted by the air service on 21 August 1917. Ticconi reached the front in January 1918 when he was posted as a sergente to *76ª Squadriglia*.

Ticconi scored his first victory on 3 May after a long dogfight, then achieved a double on 25 June with Scaroni, Lega and Mondini whilst escorting a Caproni bomber. Scaroni's view of this combat was that Ticconi seemed 'to be possessed by all the devils of hell', and he remembered that the 'boy was a marvellous fighter'. Ticconi scored one more victory with Scaroni on 7 July, shared in the destruction of an aircraft with Michetti on 14 August and claimed his final victory – a photo-reconnaissance Phönix D I, which eventually crash-landed at San Fior di Sopra – on his own the following day.

At war's end Ticconi was transferred to *81ª Squadriglia*. He was about to be discharged when his aircraft crashed at Montecelio airfield (now Guidonia, near Rome) on 26 August 1919, killing him instantly.

Romolo Ticconi's main awards – one Silver and one Bronze Medals for Military Valour

Sergente Romolo Ticconi and his Hanriot HD 1. This is possibly the aircraft in which he had a close shave on 24 May 1918 when, probably due to a short-circuit, his mount caught fire at 12,000 ft over Feltre while he was escorting a Caproni over enemy-held territory. Ticconi switched off the engine and dived, crossing the lines in a glide while flames entered the cockpit. He crash-landed near Asolo and managed to escape with first and second degree burns to his right leg. After a few days of rest he was back in action (*Ticconi Family*)

Romolo Ticconi's victories

Victory	Date	Location	Victim	Notes
1	3/5/18	Asolone	Br C I 169.78 – *Flik* 16/D, Kpl Franz Leo Sigl unhurt and Oblt Franz Weintritt wounded	With Buzio, Censi, Donati and Nannini
2	25/6/18	Mareno	Albatros D III 153.202 – *Flik* 42/J, Oblt August Selinger unhurt	With Lega, Mondini & Scaroni
3	25/6/18	Mareno	Unknown fighter	With Lega & Scaroni
4	7/7/18	Valbella	Albatros D III 153.240 – *Flik* 9/J, Zgsf Oswald Bielotter KIA	With Scaroni
5	14/8/18	Rasai	Unknown fighter	With Michetti
6	15/8/18	Colbertaldo	Phönix D I 328.04 – *Flik* 37/P Fw Gustav Franz unhurt	

1

Nieuport 11 Ni 1685 of Tenente Fulco Ruffo di Calabria, *70ª Squadriglia*, Winter 1916-17

This Nieuport 11 is finished in clear-dope overall and lacks roundels on its upper wing surfaces. The undersurfaces are painted green on the starboard side and red on the port in accordance with normal practice for Italian aircraft of this period. The serial number is edged in white and the aircraft displays the first version of the personal insignia chosen by Fulco Ruffo di Calabria – perhaps the first ever applied to an Italian fighter.

2

Nieuport 11 Ni 1651 of Tenente Luigi Olivi, *76ª Squadriglia*, winter 1916-17

This fighter has a silver/white finish and lacks wing cockades. The serial number is black edged in red, with an additional thin white line between these colours. The two black bands denote the aircraft's service with the 2nd Flight of *76ª Squadriglia*. This veteran Nieuport was still in regular use in 1918 as a trainer.

3

Nieuport 11 Ni 2123 of Sergente Alvaro Leonardi, *80ª Squadriglia*, Spring 1917

80ª Squadriglia adopted the 'Happy Hooligan' character well known in Italy as *Fortunello* ('Lucky Man') as its insignia, and several variations were displayed by the unit's aircraft. This example lacks wing cockades, although the cowling is painted in the national colours in compliance with a memorandum issued on 25 October 1916.

4

Nieuport 11 Ni 2179 of Sottotenente Flavio Torello Baracchini, *81ª Squadriglia*, Spring 1917

Flavio Baracchini adopted as his personal insignia what he called 'The Black Shield of d'Artagnan'. In the known pictures of this Macchi-built Nieuport, the shield appears to have been scratched out and replaced on the fuselage's upper decking by a comic child with a fly on his nose. The legend *non farmi saltare la mosca al naso!*, which accompanies the artwork, means literally 'don't let the fly jump to my nose!', or 'do not irritate me!'. Again there are no wing cockades present on this Nieuport scout.

5

Nieuport 17 N 2614 of Tenente Francesco Baracca, *70ª* and *91ª Squadriglia*, spring 1917

This French-built Nieuport 17 was supplied to the Italian air service in overall silver finish and without wing cockades. Flown by Francesco Baracca from January 1917, N 2614 was used by the great ace to claim his seventh and eighth victories. This was the first fighter to display the famous black prancing horse, chosen by Baracca to honour his former cavalry regiment which used a similar device in its own coat-of-arms. It is not possible to state the exact date of the insignia's first appearance, however.

6

Nieuport 17 serial unknown of Sergente Cosimo Rizzotto, *77ª Squadriglia*, Spring 1917

Maggiore Pier Ruggero Piccio, the first CO of *77ª Squadriglia*, adopted a red heart as his personal insignia. When he left the unit the heart emblem was painted directly onto the silver finish applied to all of the squadron's aircraft. Once again, no cockades were applied on the upper wing surfaces of this particular aircraft.

7

Nieuport 11, 2140 of Sergente Michele Allasia, *80ª Squadriglia*, Spring 1917

Capitano Mario Ugo Gordesco, *80ª Squadriglia's* gallant and easygoing CO, was severely reprimanded by his superiors for adopting the *Fortunello* insignia, which they considered too frivolous for a fighting formation. Units were ordered to submit preliminary proposals for squadron markings, although and this may well have been the least-respected order in the whole history of the Italian air force!

8

SPAD VII S4702(?) of Capitano Francesco Baracca, *91ª Squadriglia*, Spring 1917

The illustration used as the source for this profile does not show the aircraft's serial number, and Baracca flew several different aircraft during this period. S4702 was his first SPAD VII, being delivered to the unit on 7 May 1917. It did not last long, however, for exactly two months later, on 7 July, it was accidentally set alight during routine maintenance and destroyed by fire. This was also the day that Baracca scored his 14th victory. As with all SPADs supplied to the Italians by France, S4702's cockades have a red outer ring and green centre disc, rather than the other way round. There is no official surviving documentation to explain why this is. Perhaps, because all SPAD VII and XIIIs were imported rather than built under licence in Italy (like the Nieuport and Hanriot scouts), it was easier for groundcrews to simply overpaint the central blue disc of the French cockade in Italian green?

9

SPAD VII serial unknown of Sottotenente Luigi Olivari, *91ª Squadriglia*, Spring 1917

The outer lip of the engine cowling of Luigi Olivari's SPAD VII was painted red, earning its pilot the nickname of 'Red Devil' among *Luftfahrtruppe* airmen. The only known serial of the SPADs flown by Olivari is S4700, which was applied to an aircraft he used in April-May 1917.

10

Hanriot HD 1 French No 18/Italian serial 6614 of Sergente Guido Nardini, *78ª Squadriglia*, Summer 1917

This silver-painted French-built Hanriot HD 1 appears to display cockades rather than tricolour bands, in addition to both French and Italian serial numbers on its rudder. Note also the artistic winged devil 'cocking a snook' at the enemy in a typical Italian gesture. On 31 August 1918 the aircraft was shipped from Milan to the Poggio Renatico depot for over-haul, after which it was issued to *78ª Squadriglia*, where it reportedly remained in use through to October.

11

SPAD VII S1544 and 4707 of Tenente Giuliano Parvis, *91ª Squadriglia*, Autumn 1917
The rudder of this aircraft, which shows two serial numbers, was possibly cannibalised from another airframe, leading to a second serial being added under the original. The black colour of the crescent is confirmed by a combat report. This aircraft reached *91ª Squadriglia* on 29 September 1917, and it is likely that Parvis used it when he shared in the destruction of two German DFW C Vs with Baracca on 26 October.

12

Nieuport 17 Ni 3592 of Sottotenente Giannino Ancillotto, *80ª Squadriglia*, Autumn 1917
When forced to abandon its *Fortunello* insignia, the pilots of *80ª Squadriglia* chose the 'Star of Italy' as a replacement. As seen in this profile, the new emblem was painted directly over the fuselage roundel. Note that the red disc onto which the squadron insignia was applied had a roughly painted, or scraped, edge. The scout's serial number was marked in black, with a red and white outline.

13

SPAD VII serial unknown of Sottotenente Carlo 'Francis' Lombardi, *77ª Squadriglia*, Autumn 1917
Almost all the SPAD VIIs flown by *77ª Squadriglia* displayed the red heart marking, but rarely any personal insignia. The unit's last wartime CO, Capitano Serafini, eventually became president of the Bologna Aero Club, where the red heart symbol is still in use today.

14

Hanriot HD1 H.d. 6212 of Tenente Amedeo Mecozzi, *78ª Squadriglia*, early 1918
Amedeo Mecozzi applied markings, described in a combat report as blue in colour, to this clear-doped early Macchi-built Hanriot HD 1. H.d. 6212 was operated by the unit until 6 June, when it was sent back to the Poggio Renatico depot for overhaul.

15

Hanriot HD 1 French serial 523/Italian serial 11411 of Tenente Flaminio Avet, *70ª Squadriglia*, Spring/Autumn 1918
Patches were often used to cover holes pierced in the national colours of Italian aircraft by enemy bullets, those see in the top view of this aircraft (on page 58) could date from the 18 March 1918 action which saw Avet's mount hit by splinters from an anti-aircraft shell. It was while flying this French-built machine that the ace scored his first three victories on 17 April 1918 (all shared with Bocchese and Eleuteri). Remarkably, the aircraft was still operational in the autumn after at least six months of frontline service.

16

Hanriot HD 1 number unknown of Sergente Romolo Ticconi, *78ª Squadriglia*, Spring 1918

Romolo Ticconi chose a simple black triangle as his personal insignia, the marking being applied to the decking and fuse-lage sides of his silver-painted French-built Hanriot HD 1. In the reference photograph (see page 98) used by the artist for this aircraft, the wheel discs appear to have been painted a darker colour, which appears similar to that of the central disc of the cockade and could therefore be red.

17

Hanriot HD 1 number unknown of Capitano Antonio Riva, *78ª Squadriglia*, Spring 1918
This aircraft appears to be an unknown Italian-built Hanriot HD 1 that boasts both early and late production features. The black squadron number, red fluttering pennant and lower part of the cockade outer ring appear to be scratched or badly weathered in the photograph of this machine that has been reproduced on page 87.

18

Hanriot HD 1 HD 6252 of Sottotenente Arturo Resch, *70ª Squadriglia*, Spring 1918
Italian *Bersaglieri* regiments are elite light infantry units, famous for their plumed hats and proud *esprit de corps*. Resch personalised his late Italian production Hanriot HD 1 with the crimson collar tabs of his corps, adopting this distinc-tive colour for the fighter's headrest, upper wing ailerons, elevators, wheel discs and fin.

19

SPAD XIII S2445(?) of Maggiore Francesco Baracca, *91ª Squadriglia*, Spring 1918
The arrival of camouflaged SPAD XIIIs obliged *91ª Squadriglia* to add a white background to the personal and squadron insignia displayed by its aircraft. On his Bleriot-built fighter, Baracca, as CO, carried a small pennant, possibly in blue, on the inner struts. There were no cockades applied to the upper wings of this machine. Also shown is the image of the pranc-ing horse as it appeared on the paper seal of *Piemonte Reale Cavalleria*, which was used by Baracca in a pre-war letter to his family. If, as seems likely, the starboard side of the fuse-lage displayed the griffon, that latter would almost certainly have had a similar white 'cloud' as a background.

20

SPAD VII S6367(?) of Tenente Ferruccio Ranza, *91ª Squadriglia*, Spring 1918
Only the last two digits of this aircraft's serial number are confirmed. Examination of known *91ª Squadriglia* numbers suggests that the fighter could be SPAD VII S6367, which was initially assigned to Baracca in October 1917.

21

Macchi M.5 M 7256 of Tenente di Vascello Orazio Pierozzi, *261ª Squadriglia*, Spring 1918
The hull of this aircraft was varnished natural wood with white-painted undersurfaces. The latter usually only reached the waterline, although *261ª Squadriglia* employed this distinc-tive saw-tooth pattern on its flying-boats. Tailplanes and wings were finished in clear doped fabric, with the usual national colours displayed on their undersides. The Italian word for 'fighter' – meaning a pilot who seeks to shoot down

enemy aircraft – is 'cacciatore' (literally 'hunter' in English). Pierozzi duly painted the head of a hunting dog holding a broken Austrian seaplane in its jaws on the bow of his M.5. M 7256 was sent from Taliedo to Venice on 3 March 1918.

22
Macchi M.5 M 7242 of Tenente di Vascello Federico Carlo Martinengo, *260ª Squadriglia*, Spring 1918

The second unit within *Gruppo Idrocaccia di Venezia* was *260ª Squadriglia*, which used green and red bands to identify its aircraft. Martinengo adopted a pot-bellied winged mouse as his personal insignia. This M.5 also displays cockades on the undersurface of its lower wings – this seemed to be the case with a number of Macchi flying-boats. M 7242 arrived in Venice from Taliedo by train in March 1918.

23
Macchi M.5 M 7289(?) of Sottotenente di Vascello Umberto Calvello, *260ª Squadriglia*, Spring 1918

This standard-finished aircraft displays the green and red squadron bands, a small cockade on the wing float and the national colours on a small metal fairing on the bow. Only the colours of the Italian flag are displayed on the wing undersurfaces. See page 30 for a full description of the M.5's unusual nose art.

24
Hanriot HD 1 HD 6254 of Tenente Giorgio Michetti, *76ª Squadriglia*, Spring 1918

Michetti adopted the seahorse as his personal insignia during the war. As with many fighters flown by *76ª Squadriglia*, this late Italian-production aircraft displayed the insignia on the uppersufaces of the tailplanes (see photograph on page 64) for a short while prior to the spring of 1918, at which point it was removed. When Michetti started using a camouflaged Macchi-built Hanriot in the early summer of 1918, the personal insignia was painted in a contrasting colour to show up against the dark background.

25
Hanriot HD 1 H.d. 7517 of Tenente Silvio Scaroni, *76ª Squadriglia*, Summer 1918

This aircraft reached *76ª Squadriglia* on 9 June 1918 and was the last Hanriot HD 1 flown by Scaroni during World War 1. It was while flying this aircraft that he scored his last nine victories, prior to being wounded and shot down in it on 12 July. The personal marking and squadron number were repeated on the uppersurface of the tailplanes and in the centre of the upper wing. Scaroni had a second machine gun fitted to this late Italian-production aircraft.

26
Hanriot HD 1 serial unknown of Capitano Giulio Lega, *76ª Squadriglia*, Summer 1918

Italian pilots wore a sleeve badge (eagles for officers, winged propellers for other ranks) as well as a small gold propeller on the cap badge of their original regiment. Lega, who was formerly a grenadier, adopted a black band and stylised Italian *Granatieri* pilot's cap badge and collar tabs as the insignia for his late Macchi-production Hanriot HD 1. The badge and collar tabs were repeated on the tailplane.

27
SPAD VII S1420 of Tenente Ernesto Cabruna, *77ª Squadriglia*, Summer 1918

As per normal with *77ª Squadriglia* SPADs, this aircraft's fuselage roundel was overpainted in white and used as background for the red heart insignia, while the pilot also applied his own badge (the coat-of-arms of his hometown, Tortona). On the uppersurface of the upper wngs, the Roman numeral XIII appeared twice near the centre.

28
SPAD XIII S2438 of Capitano Fulco Ruffo di Calabria, *91ª Squadriglia*, Summer 1918

Like Baracca's 'prancing horse' insignia, Ruffo's 'skull and crossbones' was also applied over a white background. On this early Bleriot-built aircraft, only the skull's teeth remained in white, with the remaining details darkened by an unknown colour, possibly red. The presence of the griffon on the starboard side remains unconfirmed. This aircraft displays Bleriot-style camouflage and small cockades on the upper wings.

29
Hanriot HD 1 HD812 of Sergente Antonio Chiri, *78ª Squadriglia*, Autumn 1918

This silver-painted French-built aircraft reached *78ª Squadriglia* in March 1918 and was flown in combat until war's end. Like other fighters assigned to Chiri during the conflict, HD812 had an overall black tail, as described by Cerutti in a combat report.

30
Hanriot HD 1 serial unknown of Tenente Mario Fucini, *78ª Squadriglia*, Autumn 1918

At the end of the war Macchi applied this particular camouflage scheme to its Nieuports and Hanriots. The paint was applied with rags, sponges or dry-brushes in a very complex texture that could vary between aircraft and even between different parts of the same machine! On the white pennant, Fucini painted a black skull for every victory claimed. The aircraft is armed with two Vickers guns.

31
Nieuport 27 N19750 of Sergente Marziale Cerutti, *79ª Squadriglia*, Autumn 1918

Cerutti painted the letters *MIR*, which stood for *Marziale Imperatore Roman* (Martial Roman Emperor), onto the five-colour factory-applied camouflage scheme of this aircraft. N19750 also displayed the ace of clubs in the style typical of Italian playing cards – it virtually covered the fuselage serial. This aircraft reached the front in the summer of 1918.

32
SPAD XIII serial unknown of Capitano Bartolomeo Costantini, *91ª Squadriglia*, Autumn 1918

This aircraft displays a standard Bleriot-applied camouflage scheme, together with the squadron's griffon insignia. The use of Roman numerals (in black, with a white outline) to identify its aircraft was peculiar to this elite unit, and they were repeated on the fuselage upper decking too. There were no upper wing cockades on this machine. Costantini scored his last two victories flying a SPAD XIII.

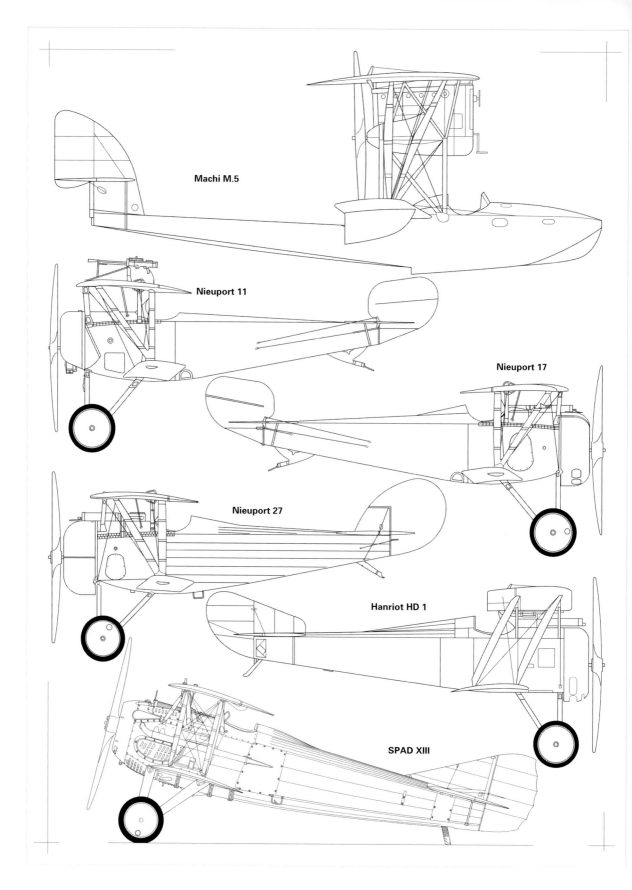

Machi M.5

Nieuport 11

Nieuport 17

Nieuport 27

Hanriot HD 1

SPAD XIII

Macchi M.5 (all drawings
on thi sspread are to
1/48th scale)

INDEX

References to illustrations are shown in **bold**. Plates are shown with page and caption locators in brackets.

Agello, Francesco 62
Albatros D III **4**, **10**
Aliperta, Sergente Gaetano **4**, 20
Allasia, Sottotenente Michele **13**, 13–14, **7**(50, 99), 93
Amantea, Tenente Antonio **14**, 14–15
Ancillotto, Sottotenente Giovanni 'Giannino/Nane' **15**, 15–16, **16**, 44, **12**(51, 100)
Ansaldo A.1 Balilla 29, 36, 71
Aosta, Duke of **16**
Austro-Hungarian *Isonzoarmee*, *Luftfährtruppe* **10**
Avet, Tenente Count Flaminio **17**, 17–18, 26, 36, **37**, **15**(52, 58, 100), **86**
AVIA L.3 45

Bacula, Tenente Adriano **68**, 76–77
Banfield, Gottfried von 30, 48, 71, 79
Baracca, Maggiore Francesco **4**, **7**, 7, 8, **11**, 11, **18**, 18–22, **20**, **21**, 27, 32, 34, **35**, 40, **41**, 46, **5**(50, 57, 99), **8**(50, 99), **19**(53, 59, 100), 69, 70, 71–72, 74, 76, **77**, 81, **89**, 89, 90, 92–93
Baracchini, Sottotenente Flavio Torello **23**, 23–24, **24**, **4**(49, 57, 99), 68, 72
Barker, 'Billy' 9
Barwig, Ltn Arnold 21
Bastianelli, Professor 24
Bedendo, Tenente Sebastiano **25**, 25
Bellingeri (naval gunner) 79
Beltrame, Achille 28
Bertoletti, Capitano Cesare **83**
Bocca, Sergente 40
Bocchese, Sergente Aldo 17, **26**, 26, 36
Boros, ZwF Franz **47**, 48
Botter, Luigi 'Bigio' **95**
Breglia, Capitano 25
Brenta, Sottotenente **35**, **38**
Bugatti, Ettore 36
Buzio, Sottotenente Alessandro 26–27, **27**, 65

Cabruna, Tenente Ernesto **28**, 28–29, 44, **27**(55, 101)
Calvello, Sottotenente de Vascello Umberto **30**, 30–31, **31**, **23**(54, 101)
Caproni Ca.3 75
Cerutti, Sottotenente Marziale 31–33, **32**, **31**(56, 101), **67**, 68, 83
Chavez, Geo 45
Chiri, Sergente Antonio **33**, 33–34, **34**, **38**, **29**(56, 101), 61, 85
Ciano, Galeazzo 37
Cik, Oblt Franz **97**
Comirato, Tenente Federico **83**
Consonni, Caporale 65
Coppens, Willy 77
Costantini, Capitano Bartolomeo 34–36, **35**, 46, **32**(56, 101), **71**, **81**

D'Annunzio, Gabriele 15, 16, 29, 63, **80**
D'Urso, Sergente 90
Dante Alighieri, RN 47
De Bernardi, Capitano Alberto 26–27, **42**, 65
DFW C V **94**
di Lomborgo, Lombardi 79
Domenica del Corriere magazine 15, 28
Dornier Wal flying-boat 75

Earl of Peterborough, HMS 71
Eleuteri, Leopoldo 17, 26, 36–37, **37**
Ercole, Maggiore **37**

FBA flying boat **8**
Fernbrugg, Fiala von 13–14
Ferrari, Enzo, and sportscars 18, 21
Ferrarin, Arturo 61
Ferreri, Tenente 80
Fornagiari, Guglielmo 'Fo-Fo' 37–39, **38**
Frew, 2Lt Matthew 'Bunty' 87
Fritsch, Kpl 67
Fucini, Tenente Mario **39**, 39–40, **30**(56, 101), 61, 85, **87**, 97

Garros, Paul Xavier 47
Goodman, Lt G A 16
Gordesco, Capitano Mario Ugo **27**, 99
Gori, Tenente **80**
Graglia, Capitano Giuseppe 14
Gräser, Ltn Franz 46, 66, **69**, 69

59, 100), **86**; 6254 **24**(54, 60, 101), **64**; 6614/No 18 **10**(51, 99–100); 7517 **25**(55, 101), **95**; 11411/523 **15**(52, 58, 100); 19209 **26**
Hansa-Brandenburg BR C I **11**, **19**, **33**
Hansa-Brandenburg W 18 flying boat 30, **31**, **47**, **48**

Il Cielo magazine **12**
Imolesi, Sergente Attilio **38**, 40–41, **41**, **83**, 83
Iskra, Fw Radames 74
Isonzo battles: 4th (1916) 41; 10th (1917) 43, 71; 11th (1917) 8–9; 12th (1917) 17
Istrana 'Air Battle' (1917) 9, 33, 39–40, 61, 64, 86, 87, **94**, 94

Josipovich, Ltn von **4**

Kauer, Zgsf Max 21
Keller, Tenente Guido 46, 74, 76, **77**
Kiss, Ltn Josef 36, 38, 87
Kowalczic, Fw Julius 14, 62

Lega, Capitano Giulio 41–42, **42**, **26**(55, 101), 98
Lenarcic, Oblt Franz **19**
Leonardi, Sottotenente Alvaro **28**, **43**, 43–44, **3**(49, 99), 88
Linke-Crawford, Frank 47, 67, 83
Lioy, Sottotenente 85–86
Lohner flying boat **71**
Lombardi, Sottotenente Carlo 'Francis' 44–45, **45**, **13**(52, 100)
Lucentini (*70ª Squadriglia* pilot) 36

Macchi L flying boat **8**
Macchi M.5 **8**, **30**, 30–31, 47, **79**; M 7242 **22**(54, 60, 101); M 7256 **21**(54, 100–101); M 7289(?) **23**(54, 101)
Magistrini, Sergente Cesare 45–47, **46**, 65, 66, **69**, 69, 81
Maly, Oblt Viktor **46**
Martinengo, Tenente di Vascello Federico Carlo 30, 47–48, **48**, **22**(54, 60, 101)
Masiero, Tenente Guido **61**, 61–62
Maurice Farman 14: **25**
Mazzini, Tenente Umberto **83**
Mecozzi, Tenente Amedeo 'Cato' **14**(52, 100), **62**, 62–63
Messina earthquake 28
Michetti, Francesco Paolo 63
Michetti, Tenente Giorgio **24**(54, 60, 101), 63–64, **64**, 94, 98
Munczar, Kpl Gottlieb 38, 74, 87
Minnichow, Vfw 80–81, 93

Napoli, RN 78
Nardini, Sergente Guido 'Rigoletto' 20, 27, **46**, 46, **10**(51, 99–100), 64–66, **65**, **69**, 69
Nicastro, Giovanni 25
Nicelli, Sergente Giovanni **38**, 66–68, **67**
Niedermayer, Ltn Josef **31**
Nieuport 10: **7**, 7, **11**, 19
Nieuport 11: **8**, 8, **11**, **16**, 19, **32**, **76**, **96**; 1451 **18**; 1651 **2**(49, 99); 1664 **38**; 1685 **11**(49, 99), **89**; 1766 **92**; 2123 **43**, **3**(49, 99); 2129 **28**; 2140 **13**, **7**(50, 99); 2179 23, **4**(49, 57, 99)
Nieuport 17: **11**, **35**, **6**(50, 99), **65**; 2139 **90**; 2142(?) **41**; 2614 **20**, **5**(50, 57, 99); 3592 **15**, **12**(51, 100)
Nieuport 17bis **23**
Nieuport 27: 8, 65; 19750 **32**, **31**(56, 101)
Novelli, Tenente Gastone 66, **68**, 68–70, **69**, 76
Nuvoli N.5 25

Olivari, Sottotenente Luigi 'Gigi' 8, **9**(51, 99), **70**, 70–72, **71**
Olivi, Tenente Luigi **27**, **2**(49, 99), 72–73, **73**
Osnago, Tenente Franco 20–21, 81
Ott, Fw Adolf **19**

Pagliano, Tenente **80**
Parvis, Tenente Giuliano (Giorgio Pessi) **11**(51, 100), 73–75, **74**
Patzelt, Oblt 67
Pessi, Giorgio *see* Parvis, Giuliano
Piccio, Tenente Colonnello Pier Ruggero 9, 11, 19, 23, **35**, 73, 75–78, **76**, **77**, 90, 93, 99
Pichl, Seekadett Franz **79**
Pierozzi, Tenente de Vascello Orazio **31**, **21**(54, 100–101), **78**, 78–80, **79**

Ranza, Generale Ferruccio 21, **20**(53, 100), 69, 72, **80**, 80–82, **81**, 93
Ravazzoni, Sottotenente de Vascello Ivo 30
Razzi (*78ª Squadriglia* pilot) 61
Reali, Sergente Antonio 36, 67, **83**, 83–84
Regio Esercito (Royal Army) 7, 8
    Aerial Gunnery School 8
    Comando Generale di Aeronautica 11–12
    Difesa di Rimini 40
    groups (*Gruppi*): *I* and *II*: 8; *III*: 8, 9, 10; *IV*: 9, 10; *VII*: 9; *VIII*: 10; *IX*: 9; *X*: 9, 10, 76; *XIII*: 9, 10; *XVII*: 10, 90; *XX* and *XXI*: 10; *XXIII* and

XXIV: 10
    Ispettorato delle Squadriglie de Caccia 9
    Istruzione provvisoria di impiego delle Squadriglie de Caccia 9–10, 11
        Massa da Caccia 76
        Piemonte Reale Cavalleria 18, 19, **20**, 100
        Sezione Nieuport 8
        3ª Sezione SVA **61**, 61
        5ª Sezione SVA 14
        squadrons: *1ª Squadriglia Caccia* see *70ª Squadriglia*; *2ª Squadriglia Caccia* see *71ª Squadriglia*; *2ª Squadriglia per l'Artiglieria* (later *42ª Squadriglia*) 72, 89; *3ª Squadriglia* see *72ª Squadriglia*; *3ª Squadriglia Aeroplani* 15; *3ª Squadriglia per l'Artiglieria* 80; *4ª Squadriglia* see *73ª Squadriglia*; *4ª Squadriglia d'Artiglieria* 89, 94; *5ª Squadriglia Nieuport* 75–76; *7ª Squadriglia Voisin* see *26ª Squadriglia*; *8ª Squadriglia Nieuport* (later *70ª Squadriglia Caccia*) **7**, 7, 19; *11ª Squadriglia* **68**; *21ª Squadriglia* 41–42; *25ª Squadriglia* **39**; *26ª Squadriglia* 23, 61, 85–86; *30ª Squadriglia* **68**; *43ª Squadriglia* 94; *70ª Squadriglia* (ex- *1ª Squadriglia*) 8, 9, 10, 11, 17–18, **18**, 26, 36–37, **37**, **1**(49, 99), **5**(50, 57, 99), **15**(52, 58, 100), **18**(53, 59, 100), 70, **86**, 86; *71ª Squadriglia* (ex-*2ª Squadriglia*) 7, 8, 9, 10, 14, 25, 87, **92**, 92–93; *72ª Squadriglia* (ex-*3ª Squadriglia*) 7, 8, 9, 10, 25; *73ª Squadriglia* (ex-*4ª Squadriglia*) 7, 8, 9, 10, 17; *74ª Squadriglia* 8, 10; *75ª Squadriglia* 8, 9, 10, 26–27, **65**; *76ª Squadriglia* 8, 9, 10, 23, **24**, 27, 39–40, **42**, 42, **2**(49, 99), **24**(54, 60, 101), **25**, **26**(55, 101), 63–64, **64**, 68–69, 72–73, 94–95, **95**, **96**, **98**, 98; *77ª Squadriglia* 8, 9, 10, 13–14, 15–16, **28**, **29**, 44–45, **6**(50, 99), **13**(52, 100), **27**(55, 101), 76, 80, 88; *78ª Squadriglia* **9**, 9, 10, 33–34, **34**, **35**, 37–38, **38**, **39**, 40, 46, **10**(51, 99–100), **14**(52, 100), **16**(52, 58, 100), **17**(53, 100), **29**, **30**(56, 101), 61, **62**, 62–63, **65**, 65, 84–85, **87**, 87; *79ª Squadriglia* 9, 10, 31–32, **32**, 40–41, **31**(56, 101), 66–67, 83–84; *80ª Squadriglia* 9, 10, 13, 15, 28–29, **43**, 43, **3**(49, 99), **7**(50, 99), **12**(51, 100); *81ª Squadriglia* 9, 10, **23**, 23–24, 27, **4**(49, 57, 99), **68**, 68; *82ª Squadriglia* 9, 10, 15, 37; *83ª Squadriglia* 9, 10; *84ª Squadriglia* 9, **28**, 28; *85ª Squadriglia* 10; *91ª Squadriglia* (later *Squadriglia Baracca*) **4**, 9, 10, 19–21, **20**, **21**, 25, 34–35, **35**, 46, **5**(50, 57, 99), **8**(50, 99), **9**(51, 99), **11**(51, 100), **19**(53, 59, 100), **20**(53, 100), **28**(55, 101), **32**(56, 101), 65, **68**, 69–72, **71**, **74**, **77**, 77, 80–81, **81**, **82**, **89**, 89–90, **90**, **91**, 92–93
Regia Marina (Royal Navy) 7, 8, 9, 30, 78–79
    Gruppo Idrocaccia di Venezia 10, **79**, 79
    squadrons: *1ª Squadriglia Idrovolanti* (later *253ª Squadriglia*) 47; *251ª Squadriglia* **30**; *260ª Squadriglia* 9, 10, 30, 47–48, **48**, **22**(54, 60, 101), **23**(54, 101); *261ª Squadriglia* 9, 10, **21**(54, 100–101); *262ª Squadriglia* 9, 10
Rennella, Sergente Cosimo 84–85, **85**
Rennella, Salvatore 84
Resch, Tenente Alessandro **37**, **18**(53, 59, 100), 85–86, **86**
Resch, Arturo 86
Resch, Zgsf Gustav **97**
Retinò, Tenente Giuseppe **8**
Riva, Capitano Antonio **17**(53, 100), **62**, **87**, 87–88
Rivista Aeronautica journal 63
Rizzotto, Sergente Cosimo Damiano 43, **6**(50, 99), **88**, 88–89, **89**
Ruffo di Calabria, Augusto 90
Ruffo di Calabria, Capitano Fulco 19, **21**, 34, **35**, **1**(49, 99), **28**(55, 101), 76, **89**, 89–91, **90**, **91**
Ruffo di Calabria, Paola 90
Ruffo di Calabria, Marquis Paolo 89

Sabelli, Tenente Giovanni 13, **80**, 80–81, **92**, 92–93, **93**
Salomone, Capitano Oreste **7**
Scanavino (*1ª Squadriglia Caccia* pilot) 7
Scaroni, Tenente Silvio 27, 39, 42, 46, **25**(55, 101), 64, 93–96, **94**, **95**, 98
Scarpis, Capitano Maffeo **7**
Serafini, Capitano Filippo 16, 100
Sir Thomas Picton, HMS 71
SPAD VII 8, 24; *77ª Squadriglia* **45**, **13**(52, 100); *91ª Squadriglia* **20**, **35**, **9**(51, 99), **71**, **74**, **77**, 81, **82**, 90; S1420 **28**, **29**, **27**(55, 101); S1544/4707 **11**(51, 100); S4691 **80**; S4702(?) **8**(50, 99); S5382 **4**; S6334 **68**; S6367(?) **20**(53, 100)
SPAD XIII: *91ª Squadriglia* **35**, **32**(56, 101), **91**; S2438 **25**(55, 101); S2445(?) **21**, **19**(53, 59, 100)
Stoppani, Sergente Mario 96–97, **97**
Szepessy-Sokoll, Oblt Rudolf 47, 74

Tacchini, Capitano Guido **7**, **71**
Taramelli, Tenente Guido **74**
Tegetthof 30
Testore, Giovanni 25
Ticconi, Sergente Romolo 42, **16**(52, 58, 100), **98**, 98
Tiscornia, Dr **82**
Trieste 73–74

Valdimiro, 2° Capo Pietro 47
Velo, Tenente 36
Vittorio Veneto, Battle of (1918) 26, 30
victory claims 11–12, **12**
Walenta, Fw Johan **39**
Wolfschutz, Ltn 40